JEWISH
HOLIDAY COOKING

13-Digit ISBN: 978-1-64643-293-6
10-Digit ISBN: 1-64643-293-2

This book may be ordered by mail from the publisher. Please include $5.99 for postage and handling. Please support your local bookseller first!

Books published by Cider Mill Press Book Publishers are available at special discounts for bulk purchases in the United States by corporations, institutions, and other organizations. For more information, please contact the publisher.

Cider Mill Press Book Publishers
"Where good books are ready for press"
PO Box 454
12 Spring Street
Kennebunkport, Maine 04046
cidermillpress.com

Typography: Justus Pro, Brother 1816, Ballinger

Image credits: page 12 courtesy of Library of Congress; pages 32-33, 42-43, 46-47, 56, 58-59, 62, 65-66, 71-72, 80, 83, 92-93, 96-97, 101, 107, 111, 119, 135, 138, 156-157, 167, 179, 182-183, 187, 197, 205, 208, 211, 212, 220-221, 227, 234, 239, 240-241 used under official license from Shutterstock.com.

All other images courtesy of Cider Mill Press.

Printed in China

Front cover image: Matjes Herring in Red Wine Sauce, page 133; Challah, page 17; Grandson's Beet & Vodka Gravlox, page 128; Chopped Liver, page 163
Back cover image: Shaved Snap Pea Salad, page 142
Front endpaper image: Shaved Fennel Salad, page 88
Back endpaper image: Matzo Brei, page 150

1 2 3 4 5 6 7 8 9 0

First Edition

JEWISH
HOLIDAY COOKING

MORE THAN 200 DELICIOUS RECIPES FOR CELEBRATING

JOSHUA KORN & SCOTT GILDEN
WITH KIMBERLY ZERKEL

CIDER MILL PRESS

BOOK
PUBLISHERS
KENNEBUNKPORT, MAINE

CONTENTS

INTRODUCTION

ORIGINS

The recipes included in this book come from Jewish families all over the world. It was of utmost importance to honor the many traditions, histories, and ethnic backgrounds that make up Jewish holiday cuisine. Many of the dishes you will discover are of Ashkenazic, Sephardic, and Mizrahi origin; but a comprehensive collection of Jewish holiday cooking would not be complete without Ethiopian, Jewish Chilanga, and Jewish Italian traditions as well.

There are also the Jewish people of India, the first group to introduce a religion outside of India's native faiths. They have lived peacefully in this part of the world for thousands of years, their numbers only dwindling after many emigrated to Israel in the 1950s. Their cuisine has blended with the recipes from their adoptive home, as so much Jewish cooking has done over time.

ASHKENAZIM

The Ashkenazi Jewish population originated centuries ago in Eastern Germany and Northern France before migrating and settling in Eastern Europe. Most Ashkenazim are originally from Poland, Belarus, Estonia, Latvia, Lithuania, Moldova, Russia, Slovakia, and the Ukraine; any references to life in the schtetl, or small village, are linked to the Ashkenazi people, as is the Yiddish language. Today, the majority of the world's Ashkenazim live in the United States, followed by Israel, then Russia. Their displacement is, of course, related to centuries upon centuries of

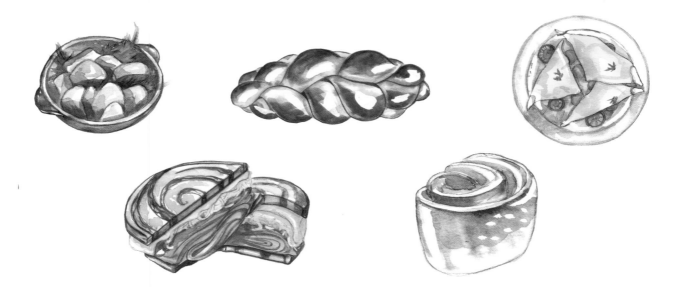

persecution. So the traditions—and recipes—that are still alive after all of these years are precious, having made their way to us after the most perilous of journeys.

When it comes to Ashkenazi cuisine, the list of renowned favorites is long. But it all starts with Schmaltz, the rendered chicken or goose fat that gives so many a dish its delicious, rich flavor. There's matzo, an unleavened bread to be eaten at Passover, and its famous offspring, matzo ball soup. For a Shabbat meal, one can expect to find roasted chicken, brisket, and plenty of carrots, beets, and cabbage, as well as dishes like kugel, kreplach, and chicken livers. The world over has come to know and love the

Ashkenazic staple that is bagels and schmear, as well as fish-heavy items like gefilte fish, lox, and pickled herring. And baked goods like challah and rugelach are beloved.

A certain corner of Ashkenazi cuisine is pure New York City. Deli favorites like pastrami, corned beef, rye, knish, and even kosher pickles (which aren't even really kosher!) are much sought-after across the five boroughs and considered iconic for any New Yorker, even though their origins remain Eastern European. But then there are the very specific traditions, like Chinese takeout on December 25, that are an invention of American Ashkenazim.

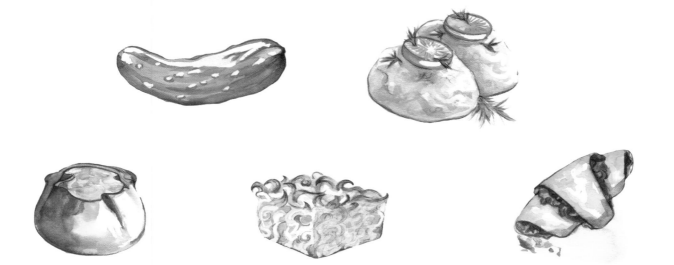

SEPHARDIM

The Sephardic Jewish population originated from the Iberian Peninsula, modern-day Spain and Portugal. Some modern scholars refer to them as Hispanic Jews, but they have dispersed across the Mediterranean since the 15th century, living in Turkey, Greece, and the Balkans, as well as the Middle East and North Africa. North African Jews in particular can be referred to as Maghrebi, and Middle Eastern Sephardim are often confused with Mizrahim, but their origins and traditions are not the same. The largest concentration of Sephardic Jews lives today in Israel, followed by France.

Sephardi cuisine revolves in part around the fresh produce of the Mediterranean regions. These vegetables are cooked, stuffed, or baked and served alongside dishes with beans, chickpeas, bulgur wheat, and lentils. Many dishes feature rice and either braised or ground meat; ropa vieja, now Cuba's national dish, is originally a Sephardic meal, for instance. And some of North Africa's delicacies, such as pickled lemons in Tunisia and Morocco, are also Sephardic traditions.

When it comes to something sweet, Sephardic desserts are rich with rose water or orange blossom, as well as cinnamon, nuts, dates, coconut, and raisins. Baklava or other honey-soaked treats are common, often served with small, powerful cups of Turkish coffee, spiced with cardamom. Flan-like puddings can also be found on many a Sephardic table, particularly sahlab, which was originally made from orchid powder, but now is mainly cornstarch and artificial flavorings.

On a Shabbat morning, expect to find bourekas, a pastry made with phyllo or brik pastry dough, as well as pastelas, a savory pastry chock-full of pine nuts, meat, and onions and sprinkled with sesame seed. And for holidays, Sephardim dip their apples in honey for Rosh Hashanah as well, but go on to have a full seder for the new year that includes dates, pomegranates, black-eyed peas, pumpkin, leeks, beets, and the head of a fish (so as to be the head, not the tail, that coming year). And, no, there aren't generally latkes at a Sephardic Hanukkah celebration, but oily, rich, fried foods are found nonetheless, such as cheesy cassola, orange-glazed buñuelos, and spinach and leek keftes, which are fried patties.

Although Sephardic traditions are slightly lesser known than their Ashkenazic counterparts in the United States, it should be noted that America's oldest Jewish congregation—Congregation Shearith Israel—is Sephardic. The congregation was established in 1654 by a small group of Jews who fled Brazil after the Spanish defeated the Dutch; they settled in a town then called New Amsterdam. The culinary traditions of Sephardim, particularly those centered around cornstarch-based puddings, have influenced American cuisine ever since.

MIZRAHIM

Mizrahi Jews, sometimes referred to as Eastern or Oriental Jews, are the descendants of the Jewish people who have existed in North Africa and the Middle East since biblical times. Far too often, their identity is confused with the Sephardic Jewish population. When Sephardim fled the Iberian Peninsula in the 1400s, many of them settled in countries where the Mizrahi population was already centered. Mizrahim then adopted many Sephardic traditions, particularly when it came to religious liturgy. So, in many ways, Mizrahi and Sephardi are incredibly similar, but their origins are different.

Today, the vast majority of Mizrahi Jews live in Israel, where, alongside Sepharim, they make up half of the country's population. Subdivisions of the Mizrahi population include Babylonian Jews from modern-day Iraq and Kurdistan, Persian Jews from Iran, and Lebanese, Syrian,

and Yemenite Jews. Some Mizrahim are also descendants of Maghrebi Jews from Egypt, Libya, Tunisia, Algeria, and Morocco. Their populations in many of these countries are nearly non-existent today; known Jewish families in Egypt, Yemen, and Iraq are sometimes recorded in single digits.

Mizrahi culinary tradition aligns with their countries of origin, however, most of these communities adopted the cooking methods and flavor profiles of their countries of choice while respecting Jewish dietary laws. One example of a well-known Mizrahi staple that results from this is the falafel. Apologies in advance for bursting anyone's bubble, but the falafel is not originally a Jewish food, rather an adopted dish from the community (likely Egyptian) that surrounded the Mizrahi people. Couscous and flatbreads from throughout the Middle East are also a staple of

Mizrahi cuisine; look for pita, malawah, and lavosh on any Mizrahi table.

The center of a Shabbat or celebratory meal in the Mizrahi world is meat. Roasted lamb or ground meat is common, usually served in an herb-dense sauce with stewed vegetables. The method of slow cooking is common in these kitchens, as well. Hearty stews that can cook overnight—particularly for Shabbat, when cooking and other work is forbidden—likely originated with the Mizrahi population. Other favorites include tebit, a chicken-and-rice dish, ingriyi, a meat dish with eggplant, and jeweled rice, a celebratory side dish "jeweled" with dried fruits and nuts.

Although quite a bit of Mizrahi food combines sweet, savory, and sour flavors, their desserts are unmistakably sweet due to the use of dates. Take, for instance, kadaif, a pastry consisting of shredded dough, crushed nuts and dates, and loads of syrup (this is a common treat found at celebrations). Mizrahim also have their own variation of charoset, which is not exactly like the Ashkenazi mixture of apples, nuts, and wine. Mizrahi charoset features, you guessed it, dates, which make the mortar-like mixture thicker and undeniably sweeter.

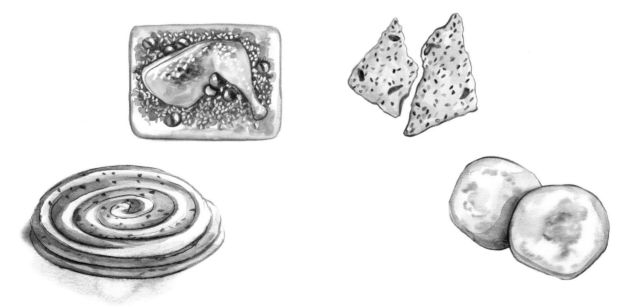

SHABBAT

WHETHER YOU SAY SHABBAT, Shabbos, or the Sabbath, this seventh day of the week—Saturday—is all about rest. Shabbat translates to "rest," and honors the seventh day that God rested while creating the heavens and the earth. Traditionally, all forms of work should be refrained from on Shabbat. For some, this means not even making a phone call; for others, it might mean simply not answering emails or doing homework, and prioritizing time with family or loved ones.

Shabbat can be broken into three different phases—and, for our sake, meals. There is Friday evening when candles are lit and dinner is served, perhaps the most popular and regularly-guarded tradition for non-Orthodox Jews. The Shabbat dinner features both challah and wine, which are blessed before the meal begins. Meat or poultry is usually center-stage at this dinner, which is meant to stand out and feel more elevated than weekday meals. A beautiful roasted chicken is perfectly welcome at the Shabbat dinner table, as is a brisket, roast, or another luxurious main course. For Ashkenazi Jews, chicken soup, brisket, or gefilte fish can be a part of the experience as well; Sephardic Jews might enjoy chicken and rice alongside roasted vegetables.

For Saturday lunch, it is traditional to have a stew prepared the night before (so as to avoid the work of cooking on the Sabbath). The Ashkenazic version of this stew is called cholent, a hearty concoction filled with meat, potatoes, and beans. Sephardim will eat chreime (fish cooked in tomato sauce), or chamin, which is their version of cholent, as well as bourekas—phyllo dough pastries filled to the brim that vaguely resemble empanadas—on Saturday morning.

The end of Saturday is marked with the havdalah ceremony, which marks the separation between the Shabbat and the rest of the week. Work is resumed for the coming days and all look forward to another coming moment of rest, delicious food, and time with loved ones. Many of the recipes featured in this book, no matter in which chapter you find them, are a perfect addition to a Shabbat table.

YIELD: **2 Loaves**

ACTIVE TIME: **1 Hour**

TOTAL TIME: **5 Hours**

2½ cups bread flour, plus more for shaping

1 tablespoon, plus 2 teaspoons sugar

3¼ teaspoons kosher salt

1¼ teaspoons active dry yeast

1¼ cups Pâte Fermentée (see sidebar), cut into walnut-size pieces

3 large egg yolks, beaten

2 tablespoons honey

3 tablespoons water, plus more if needed

3 tablespoons canola oil, plus more for coating the bowl

2 large eggs, beaten

PÂTE FERMENTÉE

French for "fermented dough," this starter needs to be made 8 to 24 hours before preparing this challah recipe.

½ cup, plus 1 teaspoon lukewarm water

⅔ teaspoon active dry yeast

1⅓ cups, plus 1 tablespoon bread flour

1 teaspoon kosher salt

1. Put the water and yeast in the bowl of a stand mixer fitted with a dough hook, then add the flour and salt. Mix on low speed for 2 minutes until combined into a shaggy dough. Cover the bowl with plastic wrap and let stand at room temperature for 30 minutes.

2. Refrigerate the mixture for a minimum of 8 hours and a maximum of 24; there is no need to return it to room temperature before using.

3. If you're measuring the pâte fermentée rather than weighing it, be sure to deflate it with a wooden spoon or with floured fingertips before measuring.

CHALLAH

Challah is a special Jewish bread that's usually braided and eaten on occasions such as Shabbat and other major holidays. Beloved by young and old, challah is more than bread, it is a deeply meaningful symbol of cherished family traditions.

1. Add the bread flour, sugar, salt, and yeast in the bowl of a stand mixer fitted with a dough hook. Add the pâte fermentée, egg yolks, honey, water, and oil and mix on low speed until the dry ingredients are completely incorporated and the yeast has disappeared into the dough. Add a little extra water if this hasn't happened in 3 minutes. Increase the speed to medium to medium-high and mix until the dough is smooth, pulls away from the sides of the bowl (and leaves the sides clean), has a bit of shine, and makes a slapping noise against the sides of the bowl, about 5 minutes. Do the windowpane test to check to see if the gluten is fully developed. The dough will look smooth and feel slightly tacky.

2. Coat the inside of a large bowl with oil and transfer the dough to it. Lightly dust the top of the dough with flour and cover the bowl with plastic wrap or put the whole bowl in a large plastic bag. Let stand at room temperature until the dough is puffy and supple, about 1 hour and 30 minutes.

3. Turn the dough out onto a lightly floured surface. Flatten slightly and divide it into 4 equal pieces (each weighing about 7½ oz.). Working with one piece at a time (keep the rest covered with plastic), form a tight log roll. Then, with two hands, give the piece a few rolls on the floured surface so that it forms a thick rope about 18" long. Repeat to make 4 ropes.

4. Leave 2 ropes loosely covered with plastic. Take the first 2 ropes and form a two-strand braid. Form an "X" in front of you with one rope going from the upper right to the lower left on the bottom, and the other on top, going from the upper left to the lower right on top. Fold the top right arm of the X down over the center so it's now facing down toward you. Fold the bottom left arm of the X up over the center so it's now where the top right arm used to be. Do the same with the top left arm and the bottom right arm. Keep building your braid in this fashion until you have no dough left to cross. Turn the braid on its side so that what was the base is now one end of the loaf and squeeze the small end pieces of dough firmly together and tuck them under the braid. Set the braided loaf on a parchment-lined rimmed baking sheet and repeat the process with the remaining 2 ropes of dough to form a second loaf. Evenly space the loaves apart on the baking sheet.

5. Carefully brush the challahs with the beaten eggs, reserving whatever egg is left over for a second egg wash. Put the entire baking sheet in a large plastic bag, or cover the challahs loosely with plastic wrap, and let them stand at room temperature until they have risen, are supple, and hold indentations when pressed lightly, about 1 hour.

6. Preheat the oven to 350°F.

7. Uncover the challahs and gently brush them again with the remaining egg wash. Bake the loaves until they're mahogany colored and sound hollow when you tap them on the bottom, 45 minutes to 1 hour. Insert a thin knife in between the strands to make sure that the dough is firm— it should have the density of a well-baked cake.

8. Transfer the loaves to a wire rack to cool completely, at least 1 hour.

CHOLENT

Consider this one of the world's oldest slow-cooked dishes, created from the necessity of not working—therefore, not cooking—on the Sabbath but still very much needing to eat. Cholent preparation can begin before sundown on Friday and be enjoyed as a hot lunch on Saturday. And while many people think of cholent as an Eastern European dish, its origins can actually be traced back to the Middle East, through North Africa, and into Spain. The end result is a plethora of cholent recipes: Iraqi tbit made with chicken, Moroccan lamb stew, and beef stew with beans and vegetables from Hungary. A simple family recipe, such as this one, is sometimes all you need.

YIELD: **4 Servings**

ACTIVE TIME: **15 Minutes**

TOTAL TIME: **24 Hours**

Cooking spray, for greasing

1½ lbs. fatty stew meat or flanken

4-5 marrow bones

2 large Yukon gold or russet potatoes, peeled and cut into chunks

1 whole onion, peeled

3-4 garlic cloves, peeled

2 cups pearl barley

1 cup kidney beans, soaked overnight and soaking water reserved

⅓ cup ketchup

1 tablespoon paprika

3 cups water, plus more as needed

2 teaspoons salt

1 teaspoon pepper

1 teaspoon garlic powder

1 lb. packaged kishke

1. Grease the inside of your slow cooker with cooking spray.

2. Add meat, marrow bones, and potatoes to the slow cooker, followed by the onion, garlic, barley, beans, and the water they soaked in.

3. In a bowl, combine the ketchup, paprika, and 2½ cups water (or beer or stock), mix well, and add to the pot. Season with salt, pepper, and garlic powder and mix well. Add kishke on top.

4. Set the slow cooker to low and cook overnight. Check in the morning and add additional water or stock if it seems dry.

ROASTED SHABBAT CHICKEN WITH
SPRING VEGETABLES, page 22

ROASTED SHABBAT CHICKEN WITH SPRING VEGETABLES

A beautifully roasted chicken with vegetables is an iconic and beloved Shabbat dinner. This recipe is simple enough to whip up when short on time, but always tastes as though it was prepared with love.

YIELD: **2 to 6 Servings**

ACTIVE TIME: **30 Minutes**

TOTAL TIME: **2 Hours**

1 (5 lb.) whole chicken, rinsed and dried well and the innards removed

½ lemon

½ white onion

3 garlic cloves peeled

¼ cup extra virgin olive oil, plus more for vegetables

1 tablespoon sea salt, plus more for vegetables

1 teaspoon black pepper, plus more for vegetables

1 bunch flat leaf parsley

2 medium zucchini, washed and cut into spears

1 bunch turnips, peeled and quartered

1 bunch carrots, about 25 pieces, trimmed

1 cup roasted onions

1. First, preheat the oven to 350°F and wash your chicken well and pat dry. Place on a rack in a roasting pan. The rack is important! It keeps the chicken from drying out and the veggies from burning.

2. Stuff your bird with the onion, lemon, and the garlic cloves. Then drizzle all over with ¼ cup oil, 1 tablespoon salt, 1 teaspoon pepper, and fresh herbs. Truss the chicken (tie the legs together).

3. Roast chicken for 1 hour and 20 minutes. Meanwhile, prep the vegetables. Clean the onions, cut the zucchini into spears, peel and quarter the turnips, and peel the carrots.

4. Toss in additional oil, salt, pepper, and herbs, just enough to coat the vegetables.

5. After 1 hour and 20 minutes, turn the heat up to 450°F to brown the chicken and add the veggies evenly on the rack.

6. Roast for another 30 minutes or so until the veggies are tender, and the internal temperature of the chicken near the thigh is 165°F and the juices run clear. Let rest covered in foil for 20 minutes.

ROASTED CAULIFLOWER

The healthy benefits of cauliflower are turned decadent with this recipe. A combination of charred, fresh, sweet, and tangy that is sure to please.

YIELD: **20 Servings**

ACTIVE TIME: **15 Minutes**

TOTAL TIME: **1 Hour**

---

8 cauliflower heads

1 teaspoon brown mustard seeds

¼ cup extra virgin olive oil

3 tablespoons Za'atar (see page 248)

2 teaspoons turmeric

1 teaspoon sumac

2 teaspoons sea salt, plus more to taste

1 teaspoon black pepper, plus more to taste

4 oz. red onions, sliced

4 oz. Medjool dates, pits removed and diced

4 tablespoons mix of chopped fresh tarragon, parsley, chives, and cilantro

¼ cup fresh lemon juice

3 teaspoons lemon zest

1. Place a rack in the middle of the oven and preheat it to 375°F.

2. Place the whole heads of cauliflower directly on the middle rack and cook for 45 minutes, or until golden brown. Do not season or rub with oil.

3. When the cauliflower is browned and roasted, remove from the oven and allow it to cool enough to break it down into florets with a paring knife.

4. Heat a heavy-bottom sauté pan over medium-high heat and toast the mustard seeds in the pan for 30 seconds, then add the oil, Za'atar, turmeric, sumac, salt, and pepper. Shut off the flame and allow the spices to infuse into the oil for 2 minutes.

5. Turn the flame back on, heat the oil and lightly fry the onions for 15 seconds, then add the dates and cauliflower florets to the pan coating and season to taste.

6. Finish with the herbs, lemon juice, and zest, and season to taste.

ROASTED CAULIFLOWER, page 23

WHITE WINE– BRAISED LEEKS

This dish is traditionally French in many ways. Pair it with roast chicken or fish, or simply enjoy on its own.

YIELD: **12 Servings**

ACTIVE TIME: **25 Minutes**

TOTAL TIME: **1 Hour and 10 Minutes**

6 large leeks

½ cup extra virgin olive oil

Sea salt, to taste

Freshly ground Black pepper, to taste

2 tablespoons avocado oil

4 shallots

2 garlic cloves, minced

1 teaspoon dried thyme

1 teaspoon lemon zest

½ cup white wine

2 cups Chicken Stock
(see page 246)

1. Thoroughly clean the leeks, trim the roots, and slice in half lengthwise.

2. Heat the olive oil in a pan over medium-high heat and season prepared leeks with sea salt and pepper to taste.

3. Place leeks cut-side down in the pan and sear until golden brown, 5 minutes.

4. Season again with sea salt and pepper and flip, allowing to cook for an additional 2 minutes, or until brown. Transfer leeks to a baking dish.

5. Preheat the oven to 400°F.

6. Add the avocado oil, shallots, garlic, thyme, lemon zest, salt, and pepper to the pan and cook until just brown, about 4 minutes.

7. Add wine and cook until reduced by half, about 10 minutes.

8. Add stock and bring to a boil. Once the mixture boils, remove from heat, and pour over leeks until they are almost but not quite submerged.

9. Put in the oven and allow to braise until tender, about 30 minutes.

FALAFEL, page 30

FALAFEL

Now known as Israel's national dish, these fried chickpea balls likely originated in Egypt. Mizrahi Jews have been eating falafel for centuries, and you can now nosh on them in countries around the world.

YIELD: **9 Servings**

ACTIVE TIME: **1 Hour**

TOTAL TIME: **24 Hours**

FALAFEL

1 lb. dry chickpeas

½ teaspoon baking soda

¼ cup tahini

1 small onion, roughly chopped

¼ cup chopped parsley

5 garlic cloves

1½ tablespoons chickpea flour

2 teaspoons salt

2 teaspoons toasted sesame seeds

1 teaspoon turmeric

1 teaspoon sumac

2 tablespoons Za'atar (see page 248)

2 teaspoons cumin

1 teaspoon ground coriander

1 teaspoon black pepper

½ teaspoon cayenne pepper

1 pinch ground cardamom

1 teaspoon baking powder (optional; makes the falafel more fluffy)

Avocado oil, for frying

YOGURT SAUCE

2 cups plain yogurt

1 green onion, minced

2 cucumbers, grated with juice

¼ red onion, grated

1 tablespoon dill

1 garlic clove, minced or smashed into a paste

1. Place the chickpeas in a large bowl and cover them by about 3" of cold water. Add baking soda and stir; this will help soften the chickpeas. Cover the bowl and let them soak overnight in a cool, dark place, or in the refrigerator. The chickpeas should soak at least 12 hours and up to 24 hours.

2. The next day, drain the chickpeas and rinse well. In a food processor combine all of the remaining ingredients, except the oil. Pulse until a rough, coarse meal forms. Scrape the sides of the processor periodically and push the mixture down the sides. Process until the mixture is somewhere between the texture of couscous and a paste. Don't over-process, you don't want it turning into hummus!

3. Cover the bowl with plastic wrap and refrigerate for 1 to 2 hours.

4. In a large deep skillet heat avocado oil for shallow frying. The ideal temperature to fry falafel is between 300°F and 325°F; the best way to monitor the temperature is to use a deep fry or candy thermometer.

5. Form the falafel mixture into round balls or patties using a 1½ oz. ice cream scoop.

6. When the oil is at the right temperature, fry the falafels in batches of 5 or 6 at a time, until golden brown on both sides. Once the falafels are fried, remove them from the oil using a slotted spoon and let them drain on a paper towel-lined plate.

7. Serve the falafels fresh and hot; they go best with a plate of hummus and topped with creamy tahini sauce. You can also stuff them into a pita with lettuce, tomatoes, pickles, and Yogurt Sauce.

Yogurt Sauce

1. Add all of the ingredients to a bowl, mix well, and refrigerate. Serve chilled.

SABICH

Israelis will happily stuff anything they can into a pita. Sure, falafel, burika, and shawarma are commonplace, but the sabich is arguably the most representative of the country's history. It was originally a dish eaten by Iraqi Jews on Shabbat morning but has now become a popular daily staple. The pita is stuffed with fried eggplant slices, hard-boiled eggs, tahini sauce, and Israeli salad—a combination of finely diced cucumbers, tomatoes, onion, and peppers. To be enjoyed on every street corner in Israel, or in the comfort of your own home.

YIELD: **6 Servings**

ACTIVE TIME: **20 Minutes**

TOTAL TIME: **1 Hour**

2 medium eggplants, sliced into 1" rounds

2 teaspoons sea salt

Avocado oil

Serve with any, or all, of the following:

6-8 Pita or Laffa (see page 229 or page 231)

8 large hard-boiled eggs, quartered

Israeli chopped salad

Tahini

Parsley

Pickles

Olives

Hot peppers

Pieces of cooked potato

Amba

1. Preheat the oven to 425°F.

2. Arrange the eggplant rounds in a single layer on a wire rack set over a baking sheet. Sprinkle both sides with salt and leave to sweat for at least 20 minutes, or up to 1 hour. Thoroughly wipe the water from the eggplant slices using a paper towel and pat dry.

3. Generously brush both sides of the eggplant with oil and place on a baking sheet, being careful not to overcrowd. Roast the eggplant for 20 minutes, flipping halfway through until browned and golden.

4. Create your spread.

SABICH, page 31

ISRAELI SALAD

The origins of the name are, like most things, a bit murky. This salad can be either Israeli or Palestinian. We like to think of it as simply delicious, all names and complications aside.

YIELD: **4 Servings**

ACTIVE TIME: **15 Minutes**

TOTAL TIME: **15 Minutes**

3 medium tomatoes, deseeded and diced

3 persian cucumbers, diced

1 red bell pepper, diced

3 scallions, white and light green parts thinly sliced

2 tablespoons extra virgin olive oil

2 tablespoons fresh lemon juice

Sea salt, to taste

Freshly ground black pepper, to taste

1. In a large bowl, toss together the tomatoes, cucumbers, pepper, and scallions.

2. Immediately before serving, season with olive oil, lemon juice, salt, and pepper and mix well. Taste and adjust seasoning, if desired. Leftover salad will keep, covered in the refrigerator, for 2 to 3 days.

ROASTED PEPPER SALAD

Roasted pepper salad is a classic Moroccan dish. Consider it the perfect accompaniment for your summer barbecues.

YIELD: **6 Servings**
ACTIVE TIME: **10 Minutes**
TOTAL TIME: **30 Minutes**

3 red peppers

2 yellow peppers

1 green pepper

½ cup avocado oil, plus 1 tablespoon

½ onion, thinly sliced

1 teaspoon white vinegar

¼ teaspoon sea salt

⅛ teaspoon ground black pepper

½ teaspoon cumin

¼ bunch cilantro leaves, roughly chopped

1. Place the peppers directly on the flames of a gas stovetop over medium-high heat, flipping them occasionally until charred on all sides and tender inside, about 10 minutes. Set the peppers aside until cool enough to handle. Peel the charred skins from the peppers and scoop out the seeds. Slice the cleaned peppers lengthwise into slices that are ¼" thick. Set aside.

2. Add 1 tablespoon of oil to a saucepan over medium heat and sauté the onions until translucent, about 5 to 7 minutes. Set aside to cool.

3. In a large bowl, place the peppers, onions, ½ cup oil, vinegar, salt, pepper, cumin, and cilantro and mix well.

4. Serve at room temperature.

TAHINI CHICKEN SALAD

Using tahini to make mayonnaise adds a nutty zip to this chicken salad.

YIELD: **6 Servings**

ACTIVE TIME: **1 Hour**

TOTAL TIME: **3 Hours**

2 (4-5 lb.) whole chickens, skins removed

1¼ cup sea salt, divided

2 sprigs fresh oregano

2 sprigs fresh thyme

4 fresh bay leaves

2 garlic cloves crushed

1 gallon water, plus more as needed

1 lemon, halved

½ cup Tahini Mayonnaise

1 bunch scallions, thinly sliced

Grated zest of ½ lemon

¼ cup Dukkah

TAHINI MAYONNAISE

2 egg yolks

¼ cup raw tahini

3 tablespoons lemon juice

1 tablespoon water

1 teaspoon sea salt

½ cup extra-virgin olive oil

To prepare the chicken

1. Remove the skins from the chickens.

2. In a large stockpot, combine the chicken, ¼ cup salt, herbs, and garlic. Add the water, topping it off with more if necessary, until the chicken is completely submerged. Squeeze in the lemon and drop it in.

3. With the heat on medium-low, bring the pot just up to a slow simmer, then turn the heat down to low, and let the chicken gently cook with the broth bubbling around it. When you glance into the pot, bubbles should be slowly floating to the top, less than an active simmer—this will keep the meat moist.

4. Check the chicken by cutting into the thickest part of the leg; it's ready when it's no longer pink at the center, about 1½ hours. When it's ready, pull the chicken out to cool; strain the broth, and save it for another use.

5. Once the chicken is cool enough to handle, pull all the meat off the bones, being mindful not to bring along the tendons or excess fat. Give it an even chop, then combine it in a bowl with the Tahini Mayonnaise, scallions, remaining ½ teaspoon salt, and lemon zest. Stir in the Dukkah shortly before serving.

Tahini Mayonnaise

1. Combine the egg yolks, tahini, lemon juice, water, and salt—preferably in a food processor, otherwise with a good whisk.

2. Slowly drizzle in the olive oil with the processor still going—or while you whisk vigorously—and continue to blend until the mixture is extremely thick and velvety. Be thorough in this step: a tight emulsion is the difference between having all those flavors hit you in equal measure or having them fall.

3. Once the mayonnaise is nice and smooth, use immediately or refrigerate for a couple of days.

DUKKAH

1 head garlic

1 large shallot

¾ cup extra virgin olive oil

1 cup raw pistachios

2 tablespoons whole
coriander seeds

2 tablespoons black
sesame seeds

2 tablespoons white
sesame seeds

1½ tablespoons whole
pink peppercorns

1 tablespoon Maldon or
other flaky sea salt

2 teaspoons ground sumac

2 teaspoons Aleppo pepper

Dukkah

1. Preheat the oven to 325°F.

2. Leaving the cloves intact, peel the garlic, trim the ends of each clove, and slice them as thinly and evenly as you can. Trim both ends of the shallot, halve it lengthwise, and thinly slice it, too. Place both in a cold pan with the olive oil, and set it over low heat until they're deep, even golden, about 30 to 40 minutes; stir occasionally, to make sure the heat circulates evenly. This is how they build flavor without any bitterness, so don't try to speed it up with a higher flame.

3. While the garlic and shallots cook spread out the pistachios on a baking sheet and roast them in the oven. Remove them from the oven when they're fragrant, after 6 or 7 minutes.

4. Line a plate with paper towels. Strain the garlic and shallots over a clean bowl, and spread them on the plate in an even layer to drain. Wipe out the pan, and fill it with the oil from the bowl along with the coriander seeds, black sesame seeds, and white sesame seeds. Toast, still over low heat, until they're crunchy and aromatic, another 8 minutes. Drain on the same plate as the shallots and garlic.

5. Add the shallots, garlic, and seeds to a large sealable plastic bag with the nuts, pink peppercorns, salt, sumac, and Aleppo pepper. Pound the mixture with a rolling pin or mallet, just until everything is roughly crushed.

CONCIA

A traditional zucchini salad that pairs sautéed or fried zucchini with bright mint and vinegar. Both earthy and refreshing, concia is a perfect starter, or accompaniment to a heavier meal.

YIELD: **4 Servings**

ACTIVE TIME: **1 Hour**

TOTAL TIME: **24 Hours**

---

3 zucchinis, sliced lengthwise into ¼" thick pieces

Avocado oil, for frying

Sea salt, to taste

Black pepper, to taste

6 garlic cloves, finely chopped

½ bunch basil leaves, finely chopped

4 tablespoons white wine vinegar

1. Salt the zucchini slices on all sides and let rest on a paper towel-lined tray for 10 minutes. Pat dry the salted zucchini.

2. Pour enough oil into a large saucepan to be ½" deep in the pan. Place over medium heat.

3. Gently place about 6 pieces of zucchini into the pan, making sure that the pieces all lay flat and do not overlap. Fry the zucchini on each side for about 5 minutes, or until golden brown. Transfer to a baking rack or a paper towel-lined tray to drain any excess oil. Continue frying the rest of the zucchini in batches.

4. Place the fried zucchini in a mixing bowl. Add salt, pepper, garlic, basil, and vinegar and gently mix until each piece of zucchini is evenly coated. Transfer to an airtight container and refrigerate for at least 5 hours, and up to 24 hours.

5. Serve at room temperature.

CRUNCHY POMEGRANATE SALAD

Symbolism aside, the pomegranate is an incredible ingredient to incorporate into your meal. The pop of each seed when bitten into followed by mouth-puckering tartness simply can't be recreated by any other fruit.

YIELD: **16 Servings**

ACTIVE TIME: **30 Minutes**

TOTAL TIME: **30 Minutes**

2 cups heavy whipping cream

¼ cup sugar

2 teaspoons vanilla extract

2½ cups pomegranate seeds

2 medium apples, peeled and cubed

1 cup chopped pecans, toasted

1. In a large bowl, beat the cream until it begins to thicken.

2. Add sugar and vanilla; beat until stiff peaks form.

3. Fold in pomegranate seeds and apples. Sprinkle with pecans and serve immediately.

FRIED EGGPLANT WITH GARLIC & CUMIN, page 44

FRIED EGGPLANT WITH GARLIC & CUMIN

A perfect example of decadent simplicity. Fried eggplant is enhanced with pungent garlic and earthy cumin to create this favorite.

YIELD: **4 Servings**

ACTIVE TIME: **30 Minutes**

TOTAL TIME: **1 Hour**

1 medium eggplant, cut in round discs about ½" thick

½ teaspoon sea salt

Avocado oil, for frying

4 garlic cloves, finely chopped or crushed

1 teaspoon ground Ras El Hanout

2 tablespoons Green Zhoug (see page 249)

1. Sprinkle both sides of the eggplant with salt, place the slices onto a tray in a single layer, and set aside for 30 minutes. Pat dry the eggplant slices.

2. Fill a large, heavy-bottomed pan with 1" of oil and set over high heat. Once the oil is sizzling, gently place about 5 eggplant slices into the pan in one layer and fry on both sides, about 3 to 5 minutes per side. Transfer the fried eggplant slices onto a paper towel-lined tray and continue frying the remaining slices in batches.

3. Plate the eggplant slices in one layer on a platter. Sprinkle the garlic and cumin over the eggplant slices and drizzle with Green Zhoug. Serve warm.

TIP: Try this same recipe using a grill instead of frying for a deeper smoky flavor.

FRIED EGGPLANT WITH MINT VINAIGRETTE

Any heaviness from the rich fried eggplant in this appetizer is offset by the light and refreshing mint vinaigrette.

YIELD: **4 Servings**

ACTIVE TIME: **15 Minutes**

TOTAL TIME: **45 Minutes**

2 medium eggplants, sliced crosswise into ¼" pieces

1 tablespoon coarse sea salt

¼ cup avocado oil, oil for frying

2 tablespoons pomegranate concentrate

⅓ cup olive oil

1 cup chopped mint leaves

1 teaspoon Ras El Hanout

1 teaspoon kosher salt

¼ teaspoon ground black pepper

1 tablespoon pomegranate seeds, for garnish

1. Sprinkle both sides of the eggplant with salt, place the slices onto a tray in a single layer, and set aside for 20 minutes. Pat dry the eggplant slices and wipe off any excess salt.

2. Heat avocado oil in a 12" skillet over medium heat. Once the oil is hot, place about 4 pieces of eggplant into the pot and fry on both sides until golden brown, about 3 to 5 minutes on each side. Transfer the fried eggplants onto a paper towel-lined plate. Continue frying the remaining pieces of eggplant in batches and add more oil to the pan if needed.

3. In a bowl, combine the pomegranate concentrate, olive oil, mint, ras el hanout, salt, and pepper and mix well.

4. Layer the fried eggplant on a serving plate, dress with the vinaigrette, and sprinkle the pomegranate seeds on top. Serve warm or cold.

TIP: Try this same recipe using a grill instead of frying for a deeper smoky flavor.

OVEN-POACHED SALMON, page 48

OVEN-POACHED SALMON

No matter how it's prepared, it's hard not to love salmon. This simple oven-poached version is a go-to weeknight favorite.

YIELD: **4 Servings**

ACTIVE TIME: **10 Minutes**

TOTAL TIME: **30 Minutes**

¼ cup mayonnaise

1 tablespoon plus 1 teaspoon sea salt

4 (6 oz.) skin-on salmon fillets, patted dry

1 bunch fresh dill, separated into 4 smaller bunches, plus 1 tablespoon roughly chopped

16 lemon wheels, about ⅛" thick

1 lemon, cut into wedges

1. Preheat the oven to 350°F.

2. In a medium bowl, whisk together the mayonnaise and salt.

3. Lay out a sheet of heavy-duty aluminum foil roughly 12" square and place one salmon fillet in the center, skin-side down. Slather 1 tablespoon of the mayonnaise mixture all over the salmon, including the skin, coating the fish evenly. Return the salmon to the center of the foil. Lay a small bunch of dill sprigs on top of the salmon and arrange 4 lemon wheels across the top in a line. Carefully fold up the edges of the foil to make a packet, and crimp the seams; this will help keep the steam inside and keep the fish moist when cooking. Repeat the process with the remaining fillets. At this point the packets are ready to cook, but they can be refrigerated overnight.

4. Space the salmon packets evenly on a large rimmed baking sheet. Bake for 20 minutes and remove from the oven. Immediately open each packet, being careful of the hot steam. The salmon will easily pull away from the skin, if desired, or it can be carefully removed whole with a flat spatula.

5. The salmon can be served hot right away, at room temperature, or cold. Sprinkle with chopped fresh dill and serve with lemon wedges.

OSHI BAKHSH

Bakhsh is a green rice pilaf that gets its color from coriander and other herbs and Oshi Bakhsh is considered the most recognizable dish of Bukharian Jewish cuisine.

YIELD: **6 Servings**

ACTIVE TIME: **15 Minutes**

TOTAL TIME: **1 Hour**

1¼ lbs. ground lamb

2 cups water

2 bunches cilantro, finely chopped

1 bunch mint leaves, finely chopped

¼-½ cup avocado oil

1½ cups basmati rice, rinsed and drained

2-3 teaspoons coarse sea salt

1 cup pomegranate seeds

1 lemon, cut into wedges, for serving

1. Place the lamb in a large pot over medium heat and add 2 cups water. Cook the meat, breaking and crumbling it frequently with a wooden spoon until it is cooked and becomes brown, about 10 minutes.

2. Add the cilantro, mint, and oil and stir well, then add the rice and salt and stir again. Increase the heat to high and bring the mixture to a boil. Cover the pot with a small kitchen towel or paper towel and place the lid above the towel. Reduce the heat to low and cook until all of the liquids are absorbed and the rice is done, about 35 to 40 minutes.

3. To serve, transfer to a wide serving platter and sprinkle with pomegranate seeds, mixing some into the rice and sprinkling the rest on top. Serve hot with some lemon wedges on the side.

RED WINE– BRAISED OXTAIL

Consider this a new weekend favorite for colder times of year. Serve this cozy dish in shallow bowls over the vegetables with plenty of sauce spooned all over.

YIELD: **6 Servings**

ACTIVE TIME: **30 Minutes**

TOTAL TIME: **3 Hours**

5 lbs. bone-in beef oxtail, cut crosswise, de-jointed

Sea salt, to taste

Freshly ground Black pepper, to taste

3 tablespoons avocado oil

3 tablespoons all-purpose flour

1 tablespoon Berbere Spice Mix (see page 248)

1 tablespoon Baharat

3 medium onions, chopped

3 medium carrots, chopped

2 celery stalks, chopped

1 tablespoon tomato paste

1 (750 ml) bottle dry red wine (preferably Cabernet Sauvignon)

10 sprigs fresh flat leaf parsley

8 sprigs fresh thyme

4 sprigs fresh oregano

2 sprigs fresh rosemary

2 bay leaves

1 head of garlic, halved crosswise

4 cups Beef Stock (see page 246)

1. Preheat the oven to 350°F.

2. Season the oxtail with salt and pepper.

3. Add oil to Dutch oven over medium-high heat. Working in 2 batches, dust the oxtail with a little flour, berbere, and baharat and brown on all sides, about 8 minutes per batch. Transfer the oxtail to a plate. Pour off all but 3 tablespoons drippings from pot.

4. Add onions, carrots, and celery to pot and stir often, until onions are browned, about 5 minutes. Add the remaining flour and tomato paste; cook, stirring constantly, until well combined and deep red, 2 to 3 minutes.

5. Stir in wine, then add short ribs with any accumulated juices. Bring to a boil; lower heat to medium and simmer until wine is reduced by half, about 25 minutes.

6. Add all of the herbs, garlic, and stock and bring to a boil; cover and transfer to the oven.

7. Cook until oxtail is tender, 2 to 2½ hours. Transfer oxtails to a platter.

8. Strain sauce from pot into a measuring cup. Spoon fat from surface of sauce and discard; season sauce to taste with salt and pepper.

9. Serve in shallow bowls with vegetables of choice, sauce spooned over.

CEDAR-PLANK SALMON

A lovely pairing of woodsy and oceanic flavors, this salmon takes on a light smokiness from grilling on a cedar plank. A classic that adds color and simple sophistication to any table.

YIELD: **6 Servings**

ACTIVE TIME: **30 Minutes**

TOTAL TIME: **2 Hours**

2 tablespoons grainy mustard

2 tablespoons mild honey or pure maple syrup

1 teaspoon minced rosemary

1 tablespoon lemon zest

½ teaspoon sea salt

½ teaspoon black pepper

1 (2 lb.) salmon fillet with skin (1½" thick)

1. Immerse a cedar grilling plank in water for 2 hours.

2. Prepare grill for direct-heat cooking over medium-hot charcoal, or medium-high heat for gas.

3. In a bowl, combine the mustard, honey, rosemary, zest, salt, and pepper and mix well. Spread the mixture on flesh side of salmon and let stand at room temperature for 15 minutes.

4. Put salmon on the plank, skin-side down. Grill, covered with lid, until salmon is just cooked through and edges are browned, 13 to 15 minutes. Let salmon stand on plank 5 minutes before serving.

MAMA KRAMER'S BRISKET

The Manischewitz or Concord grape juice not only flavors the tender, richly marbled point cut, but tenderizes each bite.

YIELD: **10 Servings**

ACTIVE TIME: **1 Hour**

TOTAL TIME: **16 Hours**

1 (15 lb.) untrimmed point- or flat-cut beef brisket

1 tablespoon freshly ground black pepper

¼ cup plus 2 teaspoons sea salt, plus more to taste

¼ cup Schmaltz (see page 247) or avocado oil

2 large onions, roughly chopped

5 large carrots, peeled and roughly chopped

5 celery stalks, roughly chopped

1½ cups Manischewitz Concord grape wine or Concord grape juice

2 heads of garlic, halved crosswise

8 sprigs fresh thyme

4 bay leaves

2 tablespoons black peppercorns

3 quarts Chicken Stock (see page 246)

1. Season the brisket all over with pepper and salt, rubbing into the grain. Wrap tightly in plastic and refrigerate for at least 3 hours, and up to 3 days.

2. Place a rack in the lower third of the oven and preheat to 275°F.

3. Heat Schmaltz in a large roasting pan set over 2 burners on high. Unwrap brisket and sear on all sides, 7 to 10 minutes per side. Transfer to a baking sheet.

4. Reduce heat to medium-high. Add onions, carrots, and celery to pan and season with salt. Cook, stirring occasionally, until browned and just softened, 15 to 18 minutes. Add wine, bring to a boil, and cook until evaporated, 8 to 10 minutes. Add garlic, thyme, bay leaves, peppercorns, and stock and bring to a boil.

5. Nestle brisket into aromatics and cover tightly with foil; braise in oven until meat is very tender but still holds its shape, 3 to 4 hours. Let cool, and then refrigerate for at least 8 hours and up to 2 days.

6. Preheat the oven to 250°F. Remove solidified fat from the surface of braising liquid; discard. Transfer brisket to a platter. Strain braising liquid into a large measuring cup; discard solids. Return liquid to pan and cook over medium-high heat, stirring occasionally, until reduced by half, velvety, and intensely flavored, but not overly salty, about 30 minutes.

7. Return the brisket to the pan, cover with foil, and heat in the oven until warmed through, 60 to 90 minutes.

8. Transfer to a cutting board and slice against the grain. Arrange on a platter and pour braising liquid over.

DAFINA

Served especially on Shabbat, this iconic slow-cooked Moroccan stew has a long history and no two variations are the same. For centuries, Jewish women around the world have prepared some kind of similar dish each week, usually prepping the ingredients Friday to be served for lunch the next day. Although recent generations have moved around the globe and reside in different countries, the tradition of this classic dish has prevailed and is a touchstone for many families.

YIELD: **4 Servings**

ACTIVE TIME: **20 Minutes**

TOTAL TIME: **24 Hours**

2 cans of chickpeas, rinsed

12 large red potatoes, peeled

2 lbs. flanken meat, bone-in

4 pieces chicken, bone-in

4 eggs

4 pitted dates

1 tablespoon sea salt

1 teaspoon black pepper

1 teaspoon paprika

1 teaspoon cumin

1 teaspoon turmeric

1 teaspoon honey

1 teaspoon cinnamon

3-4 garlic cloves

2 tablespoons avocado oil

1. Arrange the chickpeas on the bottom of a crockpot. Add the potatoes around the interior walls of the crockpot. Place the meat, chicken, whole eggs, and dates in the center.

2. Add all of the spices, garlic, and oil and mix very well but gently as to keep each ingredient in its place. Pour in enough water to cover everything by ¼".

3. Set the crockpot at a medium temperature and cook for 24 hours.

NOODLE KUGEL

Kugel is served as part of festive meals in Ashkenazi Jewish homes. In particular, it's eaten on the Shabbat and other holidays. While noodle kugel and potato kugel dishes are served at holiday meals, matzo kugel is a common alternative served at Passover seders.

YIELD: **12 Servings**

ACTIVE TIME: **20 Minutes**

TOTAL TIME: **1 Hour and 40 Minutes**

12 oz. extra-wide egg noodles

2 teaspoons sea salt, divided

½ cup unsalted butter, plus more for greasing

8 large eggs

½ cup sugar

1 lb. cottage cheese

1 lb. sour cream

2 teaspoons vanilla extract

1 teaspoon ground cinnamon

¼ cup dried cranberries

¼ cup dried cherries

1. Preheat the oven to 350°F.

2. Add 1 teaspoon salt to a large pot of water and bring to a boil and cook the egg noodles, stirring occasionally, until al dente, about 5 minutes. Drain the noodles.

3. Generously butter a 13" x 9" glass baking dish.

4. Cut the butter into a few big pieces and transfer to a small bowl and microwave until butter is melted, about 1 minute. Let cool slightly.

5. In a large bowl, whisk 8 large eggs and sugar until sugar is dissolved and eggs are frothy, about 2 minutes.

6. Add cottage cheese, sour cream, vanilla extract, cinnamon, and remaining salt to egg mixture. Whisk vigorously to combine.

7. Pour in melted butter and whisk again to combine. Add the warm noodles and dried fruit to the bowl and use a spatula to toss until coated.

8. Transfer noodle mixture to prepared baking dish.

9. Bake kugel, rotating pan halfway through, until custard has souffléed, top is browned, and noodles on the surface are crispy, about 50 minutes.

10. Let cool at least 20 minutes before slicing.

SPAYTY, page 60

SPAYTY

This is a Shabbat meal prepared by the community of Baghdadi Jews living in India. The bamboo gives this dish an earthy flavor and pleasant texture.

YIELD: 4 to 6 Servings

ACTIVE TIME: 20 Minutes

TOTAL TIME: 1 Hour and 20 Minutes

1 (3 lb.) chicken cut into 8 pieces

1½ teaspoons sea salt

½ teaspoon ground black pepper

1 teaspoon ground turmeric, divided

4 tablespoons avocado oil

3 cloves

3 cardamom pods

1 cinnamon stick

5 teaspoons ground coriander

3 teaspoons ground cumin

8 small-medium potatoes, peeled

1 large onion

1 piece of fresh ginger (2 tablespoons)

2 garlic cloves

1 teaspoon paprika

2 cups coconut cream

2 teaspoons white vinegar

½ cup water

1 (8 oz.) can of bamboo shoots, drained and cut into thin slices lengthwise

1 teaspoon garam masala

1. Place the chicken pieces into a large bowl and sprinkle and rub all sides with 1½ teaspoons sea salt, ½ teaspoon pepper, and ½ teaspoon turmeric. Set aside for about 30 minutes.

2. Place the oil into a large pot over medium heat. Add the cloves, cardamom, cinnamon, coriander, and cumin. Fry for about 30 seconds or until fragrant.

3. Place all the chicken pieces into the pot with the skin side down. Sear the chicken until golden brown, about 5 minutes on each side. Transfer the chicken onto a plate.

4. Place the potatoes into the pot with the oil and spices and fry the potatoes until golden brown on all sides, flipping them occasionally.

5. Meanwhile, place the onion, ginger, and garlic into a food processor. Process the mixture until a paste is formed, about 2 minutes. Add the paste to the pot with the fried potatoes. Add the paprika and remaining ½ teaspoon of ground turmeric. Cook until golden, about 4 to 6 minutes. Place the chicken pieces back into the pot with the skin side up. Add the coconut cream, vinegar, water, and bamboo shoots into the pot. Cover the pot and cook on medium-low heat for about 40 minutes, until the chicken is cooked through.

6. Sprinkle garam masala over the curry and serve hot.

SUMAC CHICKEN & RICE

This is an easy favorite to make for Shabbat. The brightly colored sumac adds a surprising splash of color and flavor to this simple meal.

YIELD: **6 Servings**

ACTIVE TIME: **20 Minutes**

TOTAL TIME: **1 Hour and 20 Minutes**

SPICE MIX

¼ cup sumac

Zest from 1 lemon

1 teaspoon sea salt

¼ teaspoon white or black pepper

CHICKEN AND RICE

6 pieces bone-in, skin-on chicken legs (drumstick & thigh) or chicken breast

3 cups basmati or jasmine rice

½ cup pine nuts

3 tablespoons berberis, dried cranberries, or cherries

1 teaspoon turmeric

½ teaspoon sea salt

2 tablespoons avocado oil

1 red onion, cut in ½" thick slices

1 lemon, cut in ¼" round slices

4½ cups Chicken Stock (see page 246)

Spice Mix

1. Make the spice rub by combining the sumac, lemon zest, salt and white pepper in a small bowl.

Chicken and Rice

1. Preheat the oven to 400°F with the rack in the middle.

2. Rub spice mix under the skin and on top of the pieces of chicken.

3. In a roasting pan, combine the rice, pine nuts, berberis, turmeric, salt and 2 tablespoons of oil until the rice is a beautiful yellow color. Press the rice down so it's pretty flat.

4. Top the rice with the slices of red onion and lay the chicken pieces on top of the onions. Top each piece of chicken with a lemon slice.

5. If you are assembling ahead of time and roasting later, this is the point you will want to cover the roasting pan with tin foil or lid and set in the fridge.

6. Pour the stock around the chicken onto the rice. Drizzle the chicken with a decent amount of oil.

7. Cover the roasting pan tightly with tin foil and place it in the oven. Roast for 40 minutes. Remove the foil and continue roasting for an additional 20-25 minutes until the chicken is cooked through and the rice has soaked up all of the liquids.

SEITAN BRISKET

When the family gathers for any High Holiday or Shabbat, make sure that everyone, including the vegetarians at the table, can partake. The chewy texture and savory appeal of seitan is perfect for creating a meat-free brisket.

YIELD: **6 Servings**

ACTIVE TIME: **30 Minutes**

TOTAL TIME: **2 Hours**

2 tablespoons avocado oil

2 medium onions, sliced vertically

2 medium carrots, sliced into 1" pieces

2 celery stalks, chopped roughly

½ tablespoon tamari

15 oz. seitan, sliced

1¾ cups pareve "chicken"-flavored stock or Vegetable Stock (see page 247)

¾ cup plus 1½ tablespoons grape juice or fruity red wine, divided

3½ tablespoons brown sugar, divided

1 teaspoon caraway seeds

Freshly ground Black pepper, to taste

3 tablespoons avocado oil

¼ cup unbleached all-purpose flour

2 garlic cloves, minced and divided

1½ tablespoon miso paste

1 teaspoon Sea salt, to taste

1. Preheat the oven to 375°F.

2. Add oil, onions, carrots, celery, and tamari to a heavy baking dish, stir to coat, and bake for 40 minutes.

3. Remove the dish from the oven and distribute seitan on top of the veggies.

4. In a bowl, combine stock, 1½ tablespoons juice/wine, 2 tablespoons brown sugar, and caraway seeds, mix well, and pour over seitan and veggies. Grind black pepper over top, cover tightly with foil, and return to the oven. Bake for an additional 40 minutes.

5. Remove pan, uncover, and ladle out as much of the cooking liquid as possible into a large measuring cup.

6. Add the oil to a skillet over medium heat. Add flour and cook, whisking constantly, for 3 minutes. Slowly whisk in reserved cooking liquid and stir constantly until smooth and thick, 2 to 3 minutes. If you don't have enough cooking liquid, add stock to substitute. Stir in half the garlic. Spread sauce onto the seitan, stirring to blend. Add salt to taste, if needed.

7. Raise oven temperature to broil. Prepare the glaze by combining the remaining juice/wine, remaining brown sugar, miso, and remaining garlic in a bowl and mixing well. Spoon the glaze over the seitan. Return to the oven and broil, uncovered, until bubbling hot, and deeply browned, 5 to 10 minutes. Serve hot.

APPLE WALNUT BUNDT CAKE

This fragrant olive oil cake stays moist and flavorful for over a week, so feel free to make it a few days before serving. The caramel glaze is optional, but highly recommended.

YIELD: **12 Servings**

ACTIVE TIME: **20 Minutes**

TOTAL TIME: **3 Hours**

3 large eggs

1 cup walnut halves

2½ cups bleached all-purpose flour

1 teaspoon baking soda

1 teaspoon fine sea salt

2 teaspoons cinnamon

4 large tart apples

1¼ cups canola oil

1 cup granulated sugar

¾ cup light brown sugar

2 teaspoons pure vanilla extract

Caramel Sauce and Glaze (optional; see recipe)

CARAMEL SAUCE AND GLAZE

2 tablespoons unsalted butter

¼ cup plus 2 tablespoons heavy cream

1 cup sugar, preferably superfine

2 tablespoons corn syrup

⅜ teaspoon cream of tartar (optional)

¼ cup water

2 teaspoons pure vanilla extract

1. Thirty minutes to 1 hour ahead, set the eggs on the counter at room temperature.

2. Twenty minutes or longer before toasting the walnuts, set an oven rack in the lower third of the oven and preheat to 350°F.

3. Spread the walnuts evenly on a cookie sheet and bake for 5 minutes. Turn the walnuts onto a clean dish town and roll and rub them around to loosen the skins. Discard any loose skins and let the nuts cool completely. Chop medium coarse.

4. In a medium bowl, combine the flour, baking soda, salt, and cinnamon and whisk well.

5. Peel, core, and cut the apples into ⅛" to ¼" dice.

6. Add the eggs to the bowl of a stand mixer, followed by the oil, sugars, and the vanilla. Attach the flat beater and beat on medium for 1 minute, until blended.

7. Add the flour mixture and beat on low for 20 seconds, just until incorporated. Scrape down the sides of the bowl.

8. Detach the bowl from the stand and with a large spoon stir in the apples and walnuts. Spoon the batter into the prepared pan.

9. Bake for 50 minutes to 1 hour, or until a wire cake tester inserted near the center comes out clean and the cake springs back when pressed lightly in the center.

10. Let the cake cool in the pan on a wire rack for 30 minutes. If using a straight sided pan, run a metal spatula between the sides of the pan and the cake. Invert the cake onto a wire rack that has been lightly coated with nonstick cooking spray and cool completely for about 1½ hours.

11. Drizzle Caramel Sauce and Glaze over the cake after unmolding, if desired.

    TIP: The pan must be a minimum 12 cup capacity with 10 to 15 cup capacity, or a 12-cup Bundt pan, coated with baking spray with flour; or a 16-cup two-piece angel food pan, bottom lined with parchment, then coated with baking spray with flour.

Caramel Sauce and Glaze

1. About 30 minutes ahead, cut the butter into a few pieces and set it on the counter at room temperature.

2. Pour the cream into a measuring cup with a spout and heat in the microwave until hot, then cover it.

3. Have ready near the cooktop a 2-cup measuring glass with a spout, lightly coated with nonstick cooking spray.

4. Add the sugar, corn syrup, cream of tartar (if using), and water to a nonstick saucepan and stir until all of the sugar is moistened.

5. Heat, stirring constantly with a silicone spatula, until the sugar dissolves and the syrup is bubbling. Stop stirring and let it boil undisturbed until it turns a deep amber and the temperature reaches 370°F, or a few degrees below, as the temperature will continue to rise. Remove it from heat as soon as it reaches temperature.

6. Slowly and carefully pour the hot cream into the caramel; it will bubble up furiously.

7. Use a silicone spatula or wooden spoon to stir the mixture gently, scraping the thicker part that settles on the bottom. Return it to a very low heat, continuing to stir gently for 1 minute, until the mixture is uniform in color and the caramel is fully dissolved.

8. Remove the caramel from heat and gently stir in the butter until incorporated. The mixture will be a little streaky but will become uniform once cooled and stirred.

9. Pour the caramel into the prepared measuring glass and let it cool for 3 minutes. Gently stir in the vanilla and let it cool until room temperature and thickened, stirring it gently once or twice.

HALVAH

Halvah is a confection enjoyed in many different regions and countries, but is perhaps most closely associated with the Middle East. There are many varieties, but are originally based on fried semolina. The sesame or pistachio variations are perhaps better known now, at least in North America and Europe.

YIELD: **14 Servings**

ACTIVE TIME: **20 Minutes**

TOTAL TIME: **20 Minutes**

2 cups honey

1½ cups tahini, well stirred to combine

Up to 2 cups toasted sliced almonds or other nuts

1. Heat honey on medium heat until your candy or instant-read thermometer reads 240°F, or indicates the "softball" stage of candy making. To confirm that you are at the "softball" stage, drop a bit of the honey into a cup of cold water. It should form a sticky and soft ball that flattens when removed from the water.

2. Have the tahini ready to heat in a separate small pot, and once the honey is at the appropriate temperature, set the honey aside and heat tahini to 120°F.

3. Add the warmed tahini to the honey and mix with a wooden spoon to combine. At first it will look separated but after a few minutes, the mixture will come together smoothly.

4. Add the nuts and continue to mix until the mixture starts to stiffen, about 6 to 8 minutes.

5. Pour mixture into a well-greased loaf pan, or into a greased cake pan with a removable bottom.

6. Let cool to room temperature and wrap tightly with plastic wrap. Leave in the refrigerator for up to 36 hours. This will allow the sugar crystals to form, which will give the halvah its distinctive texture.

7. Invert to remove from the pan and cut into pieces with a sharp knife.

HALVAH FIVE WAYS

It's surprisingly easy to make this confection, and family fun to customize the flavors.

YIELD: **1 Pound**

ACTIVE TIME: **20 Minutes**

TOTAL TIME: **20 Minutes**

1½ cups well-stirred tahini, room temperature

¼ teaspoon kosher salt

½ teaspoon vanilla extract

1¼ cups sugar

PISTACHIO-ROSE HALVAH

1 cup unsalted, shelled pistachios, toasted

¼ teaspoon rosewater

CARDAMOM-CHOCOLATE HALVAH

½ teaspoon ground cardamom

¾ coarsely chopped dark chocolate

LEMON–POPPY SEED HALVAH

1 tablespoon poppy seeds

1 tablespoon finely grated lemon zest

CHOCOLATE-ZA'ATAR HALVAH

½ teaspoon Za'atar (see page 248)

¾ coarsely chopped dark chocolate

Plain Halvah

1. Line an 8" x 8" baking pan or a 9" x 4" loaf pan with parchment paper, leaving a 2" overhang on 2 sides. Using a wooden spoon, mix tahini, salt, and vanilla in a medium heatproof bowl.

2. Pour ¼ cup water into a small saucepan, then stir in sugar. Attach a candy thermometer to the side of the pan.

3. Bring sugar to a boil over medium-high heat and cook, stirring occasionally to help sugar dissolve, until the thermometer registers 250°F. Immediately remove syrup from heat. Gradually stream syrup into tahini mixture, mixing tahini constantly with a wooden spoon. Continue to stir just until halvah comes together in a smooth mass and starts to pull away from the sides of the bowl (less than a minute). Be careful not to overmix or halvah will be crumbly.

4. Working quickly, scrape halvah into prepared pan, pushing toward edges; smooth top. Let cool to room temperature, then cover tightly with plastic and chill at least 2 hours. Remove from the pan using parchment overhang. Slice as desired to serve.

Pistachio-Rose Halvah

1. Place a rack in the middle of the oven; preheat to 300°F. Spread 1 cup unsalted shelled pistachios on a rimmed baking sheet. Toast until fragrant and lightly golden, about 10 minutes. Transfer nuts to a plate. Let cool, then coarsely chop.

2. Prepare halvah, adding half of the chopped pistachios and ¼ teaspoon rosewater to the tahini, salt, and vanilla mixture.

3. Stir sugar syrup into the tahini mixture and form halvah as directed. Sprinkle remaining nuts over, pressing gently to adhere. Cover and chill as directed.

Cardamom-Chocolate Halvah

1. Prepare halvah, adding ½ teaspoon ground cardamom to the tahini, salt, and vanilla mixture.

2. Stir sugar syrup into the tahini mixture, then quickly stir in ½ cup coarsely chopped dark chocolate just to combine (you want to see streaks of chocolate). Form halvah as directed. Sprinkle ¼ cup coarsely chopped dark chocolate over, pressing gently to adhere. Cover and chill as directed.

Lemon–Poppy Seed Halvah

1. Prepare halvah adding 1 tablespoon poppy seeds to the tahini, salt, and vanilla mixture.

2. Add 1 tablespoon finely grated lemon zest to water in a saucepan before making the sugar syrup, then prepare syrup as directed.

3. Form halvah as directed. Sprinkle 1 tablespoon poppy seeds over, pressing very gently just to adhere. Cover and chill as directed.

Chocolate-Za'atar Halvah

1. Prepare halvah, adding ½ teaspoon Za'atar to the tahini, salt, and vanilla mixture.

2. Stir sugar syrup into tahini mixture as directed, then quickly stir in ½ cup coarsely chopped dark chocolate just to combine (you want to see streaks of chocolate). Form halvah as directed. Sprinkle ¼ cup coarsely chopped dark chocolate over, pressing gently to adhere. Cover and chill as directed.

SALTED HONEY APPLE UPSIDE-DOWN CAKE

Milk and honey sound good, sure, but make that honey salted and now you're talking. This spin on the retro favorite upside-down cake is uplifted with just the right balance of sweet and savory.

YIELD: **6 Servings**
ACTIVE TIME: **20 Minutes**
TOTAL TIME: **1 Hour and 20 Minutes**

½ tablespoon unsalted butter

¾ cup all-purpose flour

1 teaspoon baking powder

¾ teaspoon kosher salt

½ teaspoon cinnamon

¼ cup sour cream, plus more for serving (optional)

¼ cup avocado oil

2 teaspoons vanilla extract

½ cup granulated sugar

2 eggs

¼ cup honey, plus more for serving (optional)

1 baking apple, thinly sliced into rounds (the core is edible, but seeds and stem should be removed)

Flaky salt, for serving

1. Preheat the oven to 350°F.

2. In a small bowl, combine the flour, baking powder, ½ teaspoon salt, and cinnamon and whisk well.

3. In another small bowl, combine the sour cream, oil, and vanilla and whisk well.

4. In a medium bowl, combine the sugar and eggs and whisk until foamy, about 2 minutes.

5. Gently stir in half the flour mixture into the egg mixture, then stir in half the sour cream mixture. Stir in the remaining flour mixture and then the remaining sour cream mixture until just combined. Set aside.

6. Butter the bottom and sides of an 8" cast-iron skillet or springform pan and add honey, swirling the pan around to ensure it covers as much of the pan as possible. Sprinkle with ¼ teaspoon salt.

7. Arrange the sliced apples over the honey, overlapping them to fit in the pan. Pour the cake batter over the apples and tap the pan a few times to get rid of any large bubbles. Bake until the cake is golden brown and springs back when lightly touched with your finger, about 30 minutes.

8. Let the cake cool in the pan for 10 minutes, then run an offset spatula or knife around the pan and invert cake onto a cooling rack (or unmold then invert, if using a springform). Let cool for at least an additional 20 minutes before transferring to a platter and sprinkling with flaky salt.

9. To serve, if desired, whisk extra sour cream with honey to taste, and dollop on slices of cake.

RAINBOW COOKIES

These classic New York treats are traditionally served in synagogues and at Jewish celebrations but actually have Italian roots. To make, you'll bake three thin cakes, spread jam between them and coat with smooth melted chocolate.

YIELD: **8 Dozen**

ACTIVE TIME: **1 Hour**

TOTAL TIME: **13 Hours**

1 (8 oz.) can of almond paste

1 cup unsalted butter, softened

1 cup sugar

4 large eggs, separated, room temperature

2 cups all-purpose flour

6-8 drops red food coloring

6-8 drops green food coloring

¼ cup seedless red raspberry jam

¼ cup apricot preserves

1 cup semisweet chocolate chips

1. Grease the bottoms of 3 matching 13" x 9" baking pans (or reuse 1 pan). Line the pans with waxed paper; grease the paper.

2. Place almond paste in a large bowl; break up with a fork. Cream with butter, sugar and egg yolks until light and fluffy, 5 to 7 minutes. Stir in flour. In another bowl, beat egg whites until soft peaks form. Fold into dough, mixing until thoroughly blended.

3. Divide dough into 3 portions (about 1⅓ cups each). Color 1 portion with red food coloring and 1 with green; leave the remaining portion uncolored. Spread each portion into the prepared pans. Bake at 350°F until the edges are light golden brown, 10 to 12 minutes.

4. Invert onto wire racks; remove waxed paper. Place another wire rack on top and turn over. Cool completely.

5. Place the green layer on a large piece of plastic wrap. Spread evenly with raspberry jam. Top with an uncolored layer and spread with apricot jam. Top with pink layer. Bring plastic wrap over layers. Slide onto a baking sheet and set a cutting board or a heavy, flat pan on top to compress layers. Refrigerate overnight.

6. The next day, melt chocolate in a microwave; stir until smooth. Spread over the top layer; allow to harden. With a sharp knife, trim edges. Cut into ½" strips across the width; then cut each strip into 4 to 5 pieces. Store in airtight containers.

ROSH HASHANAH

THE BIBLICAL NAME for Rosh Hashanah is Yom Teruah, which translates to "the day of shouting or blasting" or "Feast of Trumpets." With a name as festive as that, you can be sure that there's going to be some delicious food.

Rosh Hashanah is the Jewish New Year. Traditionally, it is also the anniversary of the creation of Adam and Eve. For those practicing Judaism, it is a two-day celebration where services at the synagogue can be attended and a shofar is sounded. For almost everyone, including non-practicing Jews, it is a day to gather together with friends and family for festive and symbolic meals.

The key to a Rosh Hashanah menu is sweetness. A celebration wouldn't be complete without dipping apples in honey while wishing for a sweet new year. But variations on this sweet theme are seen throughout the meal. For Ashkenazic celebrations, fluffy and always slightly-sweet challah is a must, and the beautiful and beloved bread (sometimes preferred to be served in a round shape, to represent the cyclical nature of a year) can be used to soak up the sweet-and-sticky sauce from a perfectly-cooked brisket. For dessert, nothing says Rosh Hashanah more than an ultra-moist apple cake. Side dishes featuring beets, carrots, sweet potatoes, and squash are also common as the celebration coincides with the fall season in the Northern Hemisphere. And then, there are certain classics that just can't be overlooked. Matzo ball soup, gefilte fish, kugel, and latkes—essentially, it's the perfect occasion to celebrate old, cherished traditions alongside new beginnings.

For a Sephardic or Mizrahi Rosh Hashanah, it is more traditional to hold a seder, meaning the menu features food that is highly symbolic. Everything eaten should represent prosperity and be aligned with a specific blessing. The meanings assigned to each food vary, but often derive from their name in Hebrew. Leeks, beets, green beans, and dates play an important role, as do pumpkins, other squash, and pomegranates, which represent fertility. Apples are once again included for sweetness. Historically, a head of lamb or fish could be served, but a head of lettuce can also be used to symbolize leadership, followed by a blessing where it is asked that partakers "be the head, not the tail." The menu can also include plenty of couscous, lamb, and a bounty of fruits and vegetables.

If you are looking for traditional recipes or updated versions of Rosh Hashanah classics, there is a plethora of dishes that can add that much-desired sweetness to your new year table.

MODERN HUMMUS

While stories of origin might differ, hummus is beloved and considered a staple. This recipe shows how simple this classic dish is to make—and how the flavor of this homemade dip and spread far outshines anything from the store.

YIELD: **20 servings**

ACTIVE TIME: **1 Hour**

TOTAL TIME: **12 Hours**

---

32 oz. dried chickpeas

3 teaspoons baking soda

12 cups water

12 cups Vegetable Stock (see page 246)

8 oz. tahini

2 tablespoons Za'atar (see page 247)

2 tablespoons sumac

2 tablespoons cumin

2 tablespoons sea salt

2 tablespoons black pepper

2 garlic cloves, grated

½ bunch cilantro, roughly chopped

1 cup extra-virgin olive oil

1 cup sesame oil

1 cup ice water

½ cup fresh lemon juice

1. In a pot combine chickpeas, baking soda, and water, stir, and soak overnight at room temperature, covered.

2. The next day, drain the water and rinse the chickpeas in a colander.

3. In a large pot, combine the chickpeas and stock (or water if stock isn't available) and cook at a high simmer until the chickpeas are quite soft, about 1 hour.

4. In a blender or food processor, combine all of the remaining ingredients, except the chickpeas, and puree until achieving a perfectly smooth, creamy sauce; the ice water is the key to getting the correct consistency.

5. Add the warm, drained chickpeas to the tahini mixture and blend until perfectly smooth and not at all grainy, occasionally stopping to scrape down the sides of the bowl. This blending may take 3 minutes; keep going until the mixture is ultra-creamy and fluffy, adding a little water to make the hummus move.

6. Season to taste, adding more salt, lemon juice, and/or cumin as needed.

BABA GHANOUSH

Though recipes may vary and this or that can be added to please any palate, there are some basic rules for preparing this eggplant dish. Like hummus, this spread can be enhanced with tahini and various spices.

YIELD: **12 Servings**

ACTIVE TIME: **15 Minutes**

TOTAL TIME: **1 Hour and 15 Minutes**

2 large eggplants, halved

4 garlic cloves, smashed

4 teaspoons fresh lemon juice, plus more to taste

1½ teaspoons sea salt, plus more to taste

½ cup tahini

¼ cup pomegranate seeds

2 teaspoons minced parsley

¼ cup extra-virgin olive oil

Pita Bread, to serve

1. Preheat the oven to 400°F.

2. On a sheet pan with a roasting rack, place the halved eggplants cut side up and roast for 50 minutes until they are soft when poked with a fork or knife. Remove from the oven and allow to cool for 10 minutes.

3. When the eggplants are cool to the touch, use a large spoon to scoop out the flesh of the eggplant; discard the skin.

4. Place scooped flesh of the eggplant in the bowl of a food processor, along with the garlic, lemon juice, salt, and tahini and blend for 1 minute, until the mixture is a smooth and creamy consistency. Season with additional lemon juice and salt to taste.

5. Transfer to a bowl, garnish with pomegranate seeds, parsley, and olive oil.

TIP: This is a simple iconic dish that can be prepared in a variety of ways. If you have access to a grill or open charcoal fire you can opt to char the eggplants over open flame to intensify their nutty and smoky aromas and flavors.

BABA GHANOUSH, page 77

ARUGULA SALAD WITH PICKLED BEETS

This is a bright salad perfect for almost any time of the year, although peppery arugula is usually best in spring and fall. The treat here is the vinaigrette, which enlivens all of the other ingredients.

YIELD: **4 Servings**

ACTIVE TIME: **20 Minutes**

TOTAL TIME: **3 Hours and 45 Minutes**

1 large red beet, scrubbed

1 large yellow beet, scrubbed

1 cup rice wine vinegar

1 cup granulated sugar

1 egg white

½ cup shelled raw pistachios

½ tablespoon Creole or Cajun seasoning

1 tablespoon minced preserved lemon

6 tablespoons extra-virgin olive oil

2 tablespoons fresh lemon juice

¼ teaspoon red pepper flakes

1 sprig fresh thyme, leaves finely chopped

1 pinch salt

8 cups arugula

2 tablespoons good-quality aged balsamic vinegar

Freshly ground black pepper, for serving

1. Place each beet in its own small pot, cover with water, and simmer until a paring knife can easily pierce the beets, about 30 minutes. Cool beets, peel, and slice into thin half-moons. Reserve each beet in a separate bowl to ensure that the red beet slices don't stain the yellow ones.

2. Add the vinegar, sugar, and 1 cup water to a small pot, bring to a boil and then remove from heat. Divide the hot brine between the beets; let sit at room temperature until pickled, 3 to 4 hours.

3. Preheat the oven to 300°F.

4. In a small mixing bowl, whip the egg white until frothy, then add the pistachios and spices, toss to coat, and spread on a parchment-lined baking sheet. Bake until golden and fragrant, 15 minutes. Nuts will crisp as they cool.

5. In a medium bowl, combine the preserved lemon, oil, lemon juice, red pepper flakes, thyme, and salt and whisk well. Toss the arugula in the vinaigrette.

6. Arrange the pickled beets on a serving platter and place the dressed arugula on top of the beets. Sprinkle with the pistachios, drizzle with balsamic, and top with black pepper. Serve immediately.

ITALIAN SWEET & SOUR FISH

This is a beloved Italian recipe for Rosh Hashanah. The red wine vinegar and honey combine to create that unmistakable contrast of flavors.

YIELD: **4 Servings**

ACTIVE TIME: **10 Minutes**

TOTAL TIME: **30 Minutes**

4 lbs. white-fleshed fish

1 teaspoon sea salt, plus more to taste

Black pepper, to taste

¼ cup apple cider or red wine vinegar

1 tablespoon honey

½ cup avocado oil

⅓ cup golden raisins, roughly chopped

⅓ cup pine nuts

2 tablespoons minced parsley, to garnish

1. Preheat the oven to 400°F.

2. Season fish with salt and pepper, to taste, and place in a 9" x 13" pan.

3. In a small bowl, combine the vinegar, honey, oil, and 1 teaspoon salt, mix well, and pour mixture over the fish. Sprinkle raisins and pine nuts over the fish.

4. Bake until fish is no longer translucent throughout. For a very thin fish this will only take about 10 minutes. For a thicker fillet, such as halibut, this will take up to 20 minutes. Baste after 10 minutes if the fish is not yet ready.

5. Prior to serving, sprinkle with minced parsley. Serve hot or at room temperature.

SEPHARDIC JEWELED ROSH HASHANAH RICE

This gorgeous and fragrant dish has Persian origins. It is bejeweled with various nuts and dried fruits, making it perfectly adorned for a wedding celebration

YIELD: **4 Servings**

ACTIVE TIME: **25 Minutes**

TOTAL TIME: **1 Hour and 15 Minutes**

1½ teaspoons sea salt

1 teaspoon sweet paprika

½ teaspoon turmeric

¼ cumin

⅛ teaspoon freshly ground black pepper

4 tablespoons extra-virgin olive oil, plus 1 teaspoon

1 cup jasmine rice

1 cup Chicken Stock (see page 246), plus more as needed

2 medium onions, diced

10 dried apricots, quartered

6 dried figs, quartered

¼ cup dried cherries

¼ cup shelled pistachios

1 tablespoon pomegranate juice

1½ teaspoons lemon zest

½ teaspoon orange zest

1 cup pomegranate seeds

1. In a small bowl, combine the salt, paprika, turmeric, cumin, and black pepper, mix well, and set aside.

2. Add 2 tablespoons oil to a pan with a lid over medium heat. Add the rice and the spice mix and stir well. Cook for about 4 minutes, stirring constantly and making sure the rice gets well coated with the oil and the spices.

3. Add the stock, bring to a boil, cover, and reduce heat to low. Cook for 20 minutes, remove from heat, and let it sit, covered, for 15 minutes.

4. Add 2 tablespoons oil and the onions to a pan over medium heat and cook for 20 minutes, stirring frequently, adding stock 1 tablespoon at a time to prevent from burning, if necessary.

5. Transfer onions to a plate and in the same skillet, heat remaining olive oil over low heat and add dried fruit, pomegranate juice, and pistachios and cook for 3 minutes, stirring frequently.

6. Once the rice is ready, fluff it with a fork, add onions, dried fruit, pistachios, lemon and orange zest, and toss well.

7. Right before serving sprinkle pomegranate seeds on the rice.

SHAVED FENNEL SALAD, page 88

SHAVED FENNEL SALAD

If the rest of the meal is rich and filling, you need a Rosh Hashanah salad like this one for balance. Crunchy fennel and croutons are dressed with all the acidity and zing you need, thanks to lemon juice and zest, vinegar, mint, and red pepper flakes.

YIELD: **4 Servings**

ACTIVE TIME: **20 Minutes**

TOTAL TIME: **40 Minutes**

---

2 cups cubed country bread

½ cup walnuts

6 tablespoon avocado oil, plus more for drizzling

Sea salt, to taste

3 tablespoons sherry vinegar

1 garlic clove, finely grated

¼ teaspoon crushed red pepper flakes

2 fennel bulbs, with fronds

¾ cup mint leaves

½ lemon

½ teaspoon fresh lemon juice

⅛ teaspoon chopped thyme leaves

1 tablespoon chopped flat-leafed parsley

3 tablespoon shaved Parmesan cheese

1. Preheat the oven to 400°F.

2. Place bread on a baking sheet and brush with 3 tablespoons oil and season with salt. Cook until nicely browned, about 10 minutes.

3. Place walnuts on a separate baking sheet and bake until walnuts are golden brown, about 15 minutes. Let cool, then coarsely chop walnuts.

4. In a bowl, combine vinegar, garlic, thyme, parsley and red pepper flakes and mix well. Whisk 3 tablespoons oil into the vinegar mixture, then add croutons and chopped walnuts. Season with salt and toss to coat and let croutons soften slightly; set aside.

5. Remove the stalks and fronds from fennel bulbs. Remove fronds from stalks and coarsely chop; thinly slice stalks. Place in a bowl. Cut the fennel bulbs in half and thinly slice. Add to the same bowl along with the mint.

6. Zest the lemon half over the salad, then squeeze in juice. Season with salt and toss to combine.

7. Divide reserved crouton mixture among plates and top with half of the Parmesan.

8. Arrange fennel salad over the croutons and top with remaining Parmesan and drizzle with oil.

DELICATA SQUASH PASTA WITH BROWN BUTTER & SAGE

A delicious autumnal preparation that would be welcome at any Rosh Hashanah table. The brown butter is a simple way of adding an extra layer of gourmet sophistication to this dish.

YIELD: **4 Servings**

ACTIVE TIME: **30 Minutes**

TOTAL TIME: **50 Minutes**

1 stick of unsalted butter

14 large sage leaves

½ cup panko

2 medium delicata squash, halved lengthwise, seeded, and sliced crosswise into ¼" thick half-moons

½ teaspoon sea salt

1¼ teaspoon freshly ground black pepper

12 oz. thick spaghetti or bucatini

¾ cup water

¼ cup thinly shaved Parmesan cheese

1. Add the butter to a large skillet over medium heat and cook, swirling the pan occasionally, until butter turns caramel-brown and smells nutty, 2 to 3 minutes. Add sage and fry until crispy, 10 to 15 seconds. Remove from heat. Using a slotted spoon, transfer sage to paper towels to drain. Pour all but 2 tablespoons of the brown butter into a small bowl.

2. Cook panko and 4 sage leaves in the same skillet, stirring to break up sage, until mixture is toasty, about 2 minutes. Transfer to a plate.

3. Cook squash and 3 tablespoons of brown butter in the same skillet over medium heat, stirring frequently, until squash begins to brown, about 5 minutes. Add salt, ¼ teaspoon pepper, and ¾ cup water; cover pan and cook until squash begins to soften, about 5 minutes. Remove lid and continue cooking, stirring occasionally, until liquid has evaporated and squash is tender and caramelized, about 5 minutes more.

4. Meanwhile, bring a large pot of salted water to a boil and then the cook pasta, stirring occasionally, until al dente, 8 to 10 minutes. Drain, reserving ¾ cup pasta cooking liquid.

5. Add remaining 3 tablespoons brown butter to the skillet and stir until squash is evenly coated. Add ½ cup pasta cooking liquid and simmer until a thin sauce forms, about 1 minute; season with 1 teaspoon pepper. Add pasta, tossing to coat and adding pasta cooking water as needed to coat pasta. Remove from heat, top with half of the reserved sage, and stir to combine.

6. Transfer pasta to a large serving bowl or individual pasta bowls. Top with panko mixture, remaining sage, and a generous shaving of Parmesan.

ROASTED APRICOT CHICKEN WITH MINT & SAGE BUTTERNUT SQUASH

Another beautiful recipe to add to your Rosh Hashanah table. The mint and sage add unexpected flavor and depth to the butternut squash.

YIELD: **6 Servings**

ACTIVE TIME: **30 Minutes**

TOTAL TIME: **2 Hours**

1 teaspoon cinnamon

½ teaspoon cumin

1 teaspoon turmeric

1½ teaspoons Spanish paprika

3 teaspoons sea salt, divided

1 teaspoon olive oil

1 (4-6 lb.) whole chicken

3 plum tomatoes, dice

1 cup chopped dried
Turkish apricots

4 large garlic cloves, minced

¼ cup golden raisins

3 cups Chicken Stock
(see page 246)

1 butternut squash, peeled,
cut in half, deseeded, and diced

1 teaspoon avocado oil

1 tablespoon chopped
fresh sage

1 tablespoon chopped
fresh mint

1. Preheat the oven to 375°F.

2. In a large bowl, combine the cinnamon, cumin, turmeric, paprika, 1 teaspoon sea salt, and oil and mix well. Add the chicken to the bowl and, using your hands, work the rub into the chicken, ensuring the entire chicken is coated.

3. In a deep cast-iron pot, combine the tomatoes, apricots, garlic, raisins, and stock and mix well. Place the chicken on top of the veggies and place the pot in the oven for 50 minutes, or until the chicken reaches an internal temperature of 150°F.

4. Transfer the chicken to a cutting board and let rest for 15 minutes.

5. Place the pot with the veggies over medium-low heat and simmer for 10 to 15 minutes, or until reduced by half and thickened.

6. In a bowl, combine the squash with the avocado oil, 2 teaspoons salt, sage, and mint and toss to coat. Spread out in an even layer on a baking sheet and roast for 15 minutes, or until knife-tender.

7. Using a large knife and fork, carve the chicken meat from the carcass. Cut the chicken into bite-size pieces and mix thoroughly into the simmering sauce. Remove from the heat and serve over the roasted butternut squash.

SHEET PAN TZIMMES-ROASTED CHICKEN THIGHS

A sheet pan makes this recipe both easy to prepare and a cinch to clean up. Apricots, prunes, and honey make this a sweet and savory dish perfect for Rosh Hashanah or Sabbath.

YIELD: **2 Servings**

ACTIVE TIME: **20 Minutes**

TOTAL TIME: **55 Minutes**

1 lb. bone-in, skin-on chicken thighs

½ teaspoon sea salt, plus more to taste

Freshly ground black pepper, to taste

3 tablespoons avocado oil

¼ cup fresh lemon juice, plus lemon wedges for serving

2 tablespoons honey

¼ teaspoon cinnamon

½ teaspoon red pepper flakes, plus more for serving

½ lb. baby Yukon gold potatoes(halved if larger than 1½")

1 medium sweet potato, cut into wedges the size of the potaoes

½ lb. carrots, scrubbed and halved lengthwise

1 head of garlic, cut in half crosswise

1 medium red onion, unpeeled, quartered through root end

½ cup prunes

½ cup chopped parsley, leaves and stems

1. Preheat the oven to 425°F.

2. Pat dry the chicken with paper towels. Season well on both sides with generous amounts of salt and pepper and set aside, skin-side up, on a sheet pan.

3. In a small bowl, combine oil, lemon juice, honey, cinnamon, red pepper flakes, and ½ teaspoon salt and mix well.

4. Remove two garlic cloves from the head and set aside. Arrange the vegetables, prunes, and remaining garlic on the pan with the chicken and drizzle the oil mixture over, tossing everything to coat.

5. Bake, tossing vegetables in the chicken fat halfway though, until vegetables are browned and chicken is cooked through, 35 to 45 minutes, depending on how large the thighs are; an instant-read thermometer should register 165°F. If the vegetables are done before the chicken, remove them to a plate and finish cooking chicken.

6. Before serving, grate remaining cloves of garlic into a small bowl and mix with parsley. Season with salt and pepper. Sprinkle this mixture over the chicken and vegetables.

VEGETABLE TANZIA,
page 95

SLOW-ROASTED LAMB SHOULDER WITH BRUSSELS SPROUTS & CRISPY KALE

The biggest wow factor of this impressive Rosh Hashanah roast is how easy it is to make. Rub the lamb with a mix that includes fennel, cumin, garlic, oregano, and brown sugar, then roast for several hours.

YIELD: **4 to 6 Servings**

ACTIVE TIME: **25 Minutes**

TOTAL TIME: **3 Hours and 25 Minutes**

1 tablespoon fennel seeds

1 tablespoon cumin seeds

2 garlic cloves, crushed

6 sprigs Fresh oregano

¼ cup brown sugar

1 teaspoon sea salt,
plus 1 teaspoon, divided

¼ cup malt vinegar

¼ cup avocado or grapeseed oil

1 (4½ lb.) bone-in lamb
shoulder

1 cup water

1 lb. Brussels sprouts,
trimmed and halved

½ teaspoon Freshly Ground
black pepper

½ cup smoked almonds,
chopped

5¼ oz. baby kale leaves

1. Preheat the oven to 350°F. Place the fennel and cumin seeds in a mortar and pound with a pestle until fine. Add the garlic, oregano, brown sugar, 1 teaspoon salt, vinegar and 2 tablespoons of the oil and mix to combine. Rub the lamb with the spice mixture and place in a large roasting pan. Add the water and cover with aluminum foil.

2. Roast for 2 hours, remove the foil and spoon over the cooking liquid. Roast for 40 more minutes or until golden brown.

3. Place the Brussels sprouts, 1 teaspoon salt, pepper and the remaining oil in a large bowl and toss to combine. Transfer to a lightly greased rimmed baking sheet lined with non-stick parchment paper and roast for 15 to 20 minutes or until golden. Add the almonds and kale and roast for 5 more minutes or until the kale is crisp.

4. Serve the lamb with the greens.

VEGETABLE TANZIA

This festive dish is a favorite for Moroccan Jews on Rosh Hashanah. Tanzia is a perfect way of adding sweetness to your new year.

YIELD: **6 Servings**

ACTIVE TIME: **45 Minutes**

TOTAL TIME: **1 Hour and 45 Minutes**

---

8 tablespoons avocado oil, divided

2 lbs. yellow onions, thinly sliced

1 teaspoon sea salt, plus more to taste

½ cup pitted prunes, halved

½ cup dried apricots, halved

½ cup dried figs, stemmed and halved

½ cup shelled walnut halves and pieces

2 tablespoons sugar

1 teaspoon cinnamon

Freshly ground Black pepper, to taste

1 lb. sweet potatoes, peeled and cut into 2" pieces

1 lb. turnips, peeled and cut into 2" pieces

2 lbs. butternut squash, peeled, deseeded, and cut into 2" pieces

½ teaspoon ground turmeric

½ cup blanched slivered almonds, to garnish

1. Add 6 tablespoons oil to a large skillet over medium heat. Add the onions and 1 teaspoon salt and cook, stirring frequently, until caramelized and deep golden brown, about 30 minutes.

2. Transfer the onions to a large bowl. Add the prunes, apricots, figs, walnuts, sugar, and cinnamon, mix well, and season with salt and pepper, to taste.

3. Preheat the oven to 375°F.

4. Place the potatoes, turnips, and butternut squash on a roasting pan and rub with the remaining oil, then toss the vegetables with the turmeric, and season well with salt and pepper. Spread out the vegetables on the pan and spoon the fruit mixture over and around the vegetables.

5. Add 1½ cups of water to the pan. Roast the vegetable mixture until well browned and cooked through, stirring them once halfway through cooking for even browning and adding more water if needed, about 1 hour.

6. While the vegetables are roasting, toast the almonds in a dry medium skillet over medium-low heat, stirring often, until lightly browned, about 6 to 8 minutes. Set aside.

7. Transfer the vegetables and fruit-nut mixture to a large serving platter and sprinkle with the toasted almonds. Serve immediately.

APPLE & CALVADOS TART, page 98

APPLE & CALVADOS TART

Sweet, spicy, and caramelized flavors all rolled up into one, this easy Rosh Hashanah apple dessert is the perfect excuse to practice your French (and break out the Calvados).

YIELD: **8 Servings**

ACTIVE TIME: **2 Hours and 30 Minutes**

TOTAL TIME: **3 Hours and 45 Minutes**

All-Butter Pastry Dough (see recipe)

1¾ lbs. Gala apples

2 teaspoons fresh lemon juice

⅓ cup plus ½ tablespoon granulated sugar

Calvados Applesauce (see recipe)

3 tablespoons unsalted butter, cut into ½" pieces

1½ tablespoons apple jelly

1 cup chilled heavy cream

1 tablespoon confectioners' sugar

1½ tablespoons Calvados

1. Using a floured rolling pin, roll out pastry on a lightly floured surface into a rough 16" round (⅛" thick), then transfer carefully to a large parchment-lined baking sheet. Loosely fold in the edge of pastry where necessary to fit on the baking sheet; cover loosely with plastic wrap then refrigerate for 30 minutes.

2. Preheat the oven to 425°F.

3. While pastry is chilling, peel and core apples, then cut into ⅛"-thick slices. Toss slices with lemon juice and ⅓ cup sugar.

4. Put the baking sheet with pastry on a work surface and unfold any edges so pastry is flat. Spread applesauce over pastry, leaving a 2" border, and top sauce with sliced apples, mounding slightly.

5. Fold edges of dough over filling, partially covering apples (center will not be covered) and pleating dough as necessary. Dot apples with butter, then brush pastry edges lightly with water and sprinkle with remaining sugar. Bake in the middle of the oven until the pastry is golden and apples are tender, 40 to 45 minutes.

6. While the tart is baking, melt apple jelly in a small saucepan over moderately low heat, stirring.

7. Once baked, slide the tart on parchment onto a rack, then brush with melted jelly and let cool until warm or room temperature.

8. In a bowl, combine the cream and confectioners' sugar and beat with an electric mixer until cream just holds soft peaks, then beat in Calvados.

9. Serve tart topped with dollops of Calvados cream.

ALL-BUTTER PASTRY DOUGH

Use this for any and all pies.

YIELD: **1 Pie Crust**
ACTIVE TIME: **20 Minutes**
TOTAL TIME: **1 Hour and 20 Minutes**

2½ cups all-purpose flour
(not unbleached)

2 teaspoons sugar

¾ teaspoon sea salt

2 sticks of cold unsalted butter,
cut into ½" pieces

9-12 tablespoons ice water

1. In a bowl, combine the flour, sugar, and salt, whisk well, and then blend in butter with your fingertips or a pastry blender (or pulse in a food processor) just until most of the mixture resembles coarse meal with small (roughly pea-size) butter lumps.

2. Drizzle 9 tablespoons ice water evenly over the mixture and gently stir with a fork (or pulse in the food processor) until incorporated.

3. Squeeze a small handful. If it doesn't hold together, add more ice water 1 tablespoon at a time, stirring (or pulsing) until just incorporated, then test again. Do not overwork the mixture, or pastry will be tough.

4. Turn out mixture onto a lightly floured surface and divide into 8 portions. With the heel of your hand, smear each portion once or twice in a forward motion to help distribute fat. Gather dough together with a bench scraper and press into a ball, then flatten into a 6" disk. Refrigerate dough, wrapped in plastic wrap, until firm, at least 1 hour.

CALVADOS APPLESAUCE

If you like applesauce, and you like Calvados, you'll love this, which works as both a dessert and a sweet side dish.

YIELD: **6 Servings**
ACTIVE TIME: **25 Minutes**
TOTAL TIME: **45 Minutes**

1 lb. Gala apples

½ cup water

½ cup sugar

½ teaspoon lemon zest

1/8 teaspoon cinnamon

2 tablespoons Calvados

1. Peel and core apples, then cut into 1" pieces.

2. Add apples, water, sugar, zest, and cinnamon to a saucepan over medium-high heat and bring to a boil, stirring occasionally, then reduce heat and simmer, covered, for 15 minutes.

3. Remove the lid and simmer until most of the liquid is evaporated, 5 to 10 minutes. Add Calvados and simmer, stirring occasionally, 1 minute. Mash apples with a potato masher or a fork to a coarse sauce, then remove from heat and let cool.

APPLE CAKE

L'shanah tovah! If you want your new year—and Rosh Hashanah celebration—to be truly sweet, you're going to need a lot of apples. This apple cake recipe is the kind you keep in your back pocket for celebrations, no matter the time of year.

YIELD: **9 Servings**
ACTIVE TIME: **10 Minutes**
TOTAL TIME: **1 Hour and 10 Minutes**

¾ cup unsalted butter, softened and divided

1½ cups sugar, divided

1 egg

1 teaspoon vanilla extract

1 cup all-purpose flour

1 teaspoon baking soda

½ teaspoon cinnamon

¼ teaspoon salt

¼ teaspoon nutmeg

2 medium tart apples, peeled and grated

½ cup chopped walnuts

½ cup packed brown sugar

½ cup half-and-half cream

1. Preheat the oven to 350°F.

2. In a large bowl, cream ¼ cup butter and 1 cup sugar. Beat in egg and vanilla.

3. In a separate bowl, combine flour, baking soda, cinnamon, salt and nutmeg, mix well, and gradually add to the creamed mixture. Stir in apples and walnuts.

4. Pour the batter into a greased 8" circular baking dish. Bake for 40 to 45 minutes, or until a toothpick inserted in the center comes out clean.

5. Meanwhile, add the remaining butter to a saucepan over medium heat. Once the butter is melted, stir in the remaining sugar, brown sugar, and cream and bring to a boil, stirring constantly. Reduce heat and simmer, uncovered, for 15 minutes, stirring occasionally. Serve over warm cake.

GOLDEN BROWN COOKIES WITH APPLE FILLING

Why should apple cakes have all the fun? These cookies are a delicious alternative for a Rosh Hashanah treat.

YIELD: **24 Cookies**

ACTIVE TIME: **20 Minutes**

TOTAL TIME: **30 Minutes**

---

10 tablespoons unsalted butter, soft

1 cup dark brown sugar

1 large egg, room temperature

1 teaspoon vanilla extract

½ teaspoon sea salt

2 cups all-purpose flour

½ teaspoon baking soda

½ teaspoon baking powder

1 small Granny Smith apple, peeled and diced

1 cup craisins

1 cup walnuts pieces

CINNAMON-SUGAR MIXTURE

3 tablespoon granulated white sugar

¼ teaspoon ginger

2 teaspoons cinnamon

¼ teaspoon ground cloves

½ teaspoon nutmeg

1. Preheat the oven to 375°F. Cream butter until smooth, add brown sugar and cream further.

2. Add egg, vanilla, salt, cinnamon, and cloves and mix until light and creamy.

3. Sift together flour, baking soda, and baking powder. Add flour mixture in one step to creamed mixture and mix until just combined, do not over mix.

4. Mix into cookie batter along with craisins and walnuts.

5. Scoop dough using a medium size ice cream scoop and set aside.

6. In a bowl, combine and mix well.

7. Roll each ball in the sugar/cinnamon mixture.

8. Place on the parchment-covered baking sheet about 2" apart and slightly flatten.

9. Bake at 350°F for 12 minutes. Do not over bake; they will be a little soft when they are removed from the oven but they will harden.

HONEY CAKE

With its velvety chocolate glaze and snowy flakes of sea salt, this dressed-up honey cake is perfect for Rosh Hashanah.

YIELD: **1 (10") Cake**

ACTIVE TIME: **1 Hour**

TOTAL TIME: **4 Hours**

CAKE

Baking spray

2½ cups all-purpose flour

2 teaspoons baking powder

½ teaspoon baking soda

½ teaspoon salt

2 teaspoons cinnamon

¼ teaspoon ground ginger

¼ teaspoon ground clove

3 large eggs

1 cup sugar

1¼ cups avocado oil

1 cup pure honey

¾ cup lukewarm coffee (brewed, or instant dissolved in water)

1½ teaspoons packed grated orange zest

CHOCOLATE GLAZE

¼ cup plus 2 tablespoons well-stirred canned unsweetened coconut milk (not light)

2 teaspoons light corn syrup

4 oz. bittersweet (60% cacao) chocolate, finely chopped

Garnish

Flaky sea salt, such as Maldon (optional)

Cake

1. Heat oven to 350°F with rack in middle. Generously spray pan, including center tube, with baking spray.

2. Whisk together flour, baking powder and soda, salt, and spices in a large bowl.

3. Whisk eggs well in another large bowl and whisk in sugar, oil, honey, coffee, and zest until well combined.

4. Make a well in the center of the flour mixture and add the honey mixture, then stir with the whisk until the batter is smooth.

5. Pour batter into pan and bake in the oven until springy to the touch and a cake tester comes out clean, 45 to 50 minutes.

6. Let the cake cool in the pan on a rack for 20 minutes.

7. Loosen the cake from the pan with a thin rubber spatula, then invert cake onto the rack and cool completely.

Chocolate Glaze

1. Bring coconut milk and corn syrup to a simmer in a small heavy pan, stirring until combined.

2. Remove pan from heat and add chocolate. Let chocolate stand 1 minute, then stir until chocolate is melted and glaze is smooth.

3. Let glaze stand, stirring occasionally, until thickened slightly, but still pourable.

4. Transfer cake to a cake plate and slowly pour the chocolate glaze over the top of the cake, letting it drip down the sides. If desired, let the cake stand at room temperature until glaze is set.

5. Just before serving, sprinkle glaze lightly with flaky sea salt, if using.

TIP: Measuring oil and honey: Both should be measured in a liquid measuring cup. The oil is listed first, because if you measure the honey in it afterward, without washing the cup, the honey will slide out easily, with barely any help needed from a rubber spatula.

INVERTING THE CAKE ONTO A RACK: The best way to do this is to place a rack over the top of the pan, then, holding the rack and pan together, flip the cake pan and rack over so that the cake can slide safely out of the pan onto the rack.

CHOPPING CHOCOLATE: The easiest way to chop chocolate is with a long serrated bread knife. Or you can break the chocolate into squares (if you are using a bar) and pulse it in a food processor.

HONEY POMEGRANATE CAKE

May dry honey cakes be forever banished from your Rosh Hashanah table! This version with the oh-so important addition of pomegranate is sure to be a favorite.

YIELD: **4 Servings**

ACTIVE TIME: **10 Minutes**

TOTAL TIME: **1 Hour**

CAKE

4 eggs

1 cup sugar

1 cup canola oil

1 cup cold brewed pomegranate tea (brewed for 30 minutes)

1½ cups honey

3 cups flour

3 teaspoons baking powder

½ teaspoon baking soda

GLAZE

½ cup pomegranate juice

¼ cup sugar

Juice of ½ lemon

4 tablespoons powdered sugar

¼ cup pomegranate seeds

1. Using a hand mixer or a stand mixer to beat eggs and sugar until smooth. Add oil, brewed tea, and honey and mix well.

2. In a separate bowl, combine dry ingredients and slowly add to liquid ingredients. Pour into a 10" ungreased angel food cake pan, not a bundt pan.

3. Preheat the oven to 350°F. Bake for 15 minutes then reduce heat to 300°F and bake for an additional 45 minutes.

4. When the cake is done invert and allow to cool completely before removing.

5. For the glaze, combine pomegranate juice, sugar, and lemon juice in a small pot over medium heat. Bring to a boil then let simmer uncovered for 15 minutes, stirring frequently. It will become syrup and reduce to about half. Remove from heat, let cool slightly, and whisk in powdered sugar until smooth.

6. Stir in pomegranate seeds and pour over the cake.

SFRATTI

Not only do we have Jewish-Italian grandmothers to thank for sfratti, but also the original Sephardic population that settled in Italy while fleeing the Spanish Inquisition. Originating in Pitigliano, a medieval Tuscan village that was considered by its Jewish inhabitants to be a Little Jerusalem, "sfratti" means eviction—which all Pitigliano Jews faced before settling there. These rod-shaped cookies are now eaten on Rosh Hashanah to ward off further evictions.

YIELD: **6 Servings**

ACTIVE TIME: **30 Minutes**

TOTAL TIME: **3 Hours**

1 large egg beaten with
1 tablespoon water

¼ teaspoon freshly grated
black pepper

dash of nutmeg

¼ teaspoon ground ginger

¾ teaspoon ground cinnamon

2 teaspoons grated orange zest

2 cups chopped walnuts

1 cup honey

⅔ cup chilled dry white wine

⅓ cup cold, unsalted butter

1 pinch salt

1 cup sugar

3 cups unbleached,
all-purpose flour

1. Combine flour, sugar, and salt in a medium bowl. Cut in the butter until it resembles coarse crumbs. Add the wine a little at a time, mixing with a fork to moisten the dough. Continue adding wine until the dough just holds together. Divide dough in half and press into balls. Flatten balls into discs, then wrap and refrigerate for at least an hour.

2. Dough can be made up to 3 days ahead. When ready to use, allow dough to stand at room temperature until malleable but not soft.

3. In a medium saucepan over medium heat, bring the honey for the filling to a boil and cook for 5 minutes. If it starts to foam over, lower heat slightly. Add remaining ingredients and cook, stirring constantly for another 3 to 5 minutes, then remove from heat. If the mixture begins to turn dark, it is starting to burn—remove from the heat immediately and keep stirring!

4. Let the mixture stand, stirring occasionally, until it is cool enough to handle. Pour mixture onto a floured surface, divide into 6 equal portions, and shape the portions into 14" long sticks.

5. Preheat the oven to 350°F. Line a large baking sheet with parchment paper.

6. On a piece of waxed paper or plastic wrap or on a lightly floured surface, roll each disc of dough into a 14" x 12" rectangle, then cut each rectangle lengthwise into three long rectangles. Place one of the strips of filling near a long side of each rectangle, then roll the dough around the filling.

7. You will have six long sticks of dough with filling in each. Cut these into 2" sticks. Place seam side down on the prepared baking sheet, leaving 1" between the cookies. Brush with the egg wash.

8. Bake cookies until golden, about 20 minutes. Transfer to a rack and let cool.

PUMPKIN CRANBERRY CUPCAKES

Right on time for autumn baking, these cupcakes are a fun addition to your Rosh Hashanah celebration. Pumpkins and squash are symbolic New Year's staples, and one can pray that their good deeds "call out their merit" before consuming them.

YIELD: **12 Cupcakes**

ACTIVE TIME: **15 Minutes**

TOTAL TIME: **35 Minutes**

1 (15 oz.) can of pumpkin puree

1 egg

1 teaspoon vanilla

½ cup unsalted butter, softened

½ cup granulated sugar

1½ teaspoons ground cinnamon

1 pinch nutmeg

½ cup packed light brown sugar

1 teaspoon ginger

1 teaspoon baking soda

1½ teaspoons baking powder

½ cup dried cranberries

2 cups all-purpose flour

1. Preheat the oven to 350°F and line a cupcake pan with paper or silicone liners. In a bowl, whisk together the flour, baking soda and powder, and spices; set aside. In a separate bowl, cream the sugars and butter together until fluffy. Add the eggs, vanilla, and pumpkin puree, stirring until fully combined. Fold in the cranberries.

2. Slowly add the dry ingredients to the wet, stirring until just combined. Pour batter into prepared cupcake tins, filling each tin approximately ¾ full. Bake for 20 to 25 minutes until a tester comes out clean. Allow to fully cool, then frost as desired or sprinkle with confectioners sugar.

YEASTED APPLE COFFEE CAKE

Another apple dessert essential for Rosh Hashanah. Jump right into fall baking with this flavorful, bready cake topped with tart apple slices and an irresistible cinnamon-oat streusel.

YIELD: **12 Servings**

ACTIVE TIME: **30 Minutes**

TOTAL TIME: **3 Hours**

CAKE

6 tablespoons unsalted butter, melted, slightly cooled, plus more

1¼ oz. envelope active dry yeast (about 2¼ teaspoons)

⅔ cup (packed) light brown sugar, divided

1 large egg, room temperature

3 cups all-purpose flour, divided

½ cup sour cream, room temperature

2 teaspoons finely grated orange zest

⅓ cup fresh orange juice

2 teaspoons baking powder

1 teaspoon sea salt

STREUSEL

½ cup all-purpose flour

½ cup old-fashioned oats

⅓ cup (packed) light brown sugar

2 tablespoons granulated sugar

1 teaspoon ground cinnamon

Sea salt, to taste

6 tablespoons unsalted butter, melted, slightly cooled

2 lbs. firm baking apples, halved, cored, very thinly sliced

1½ cups powdered sugar

2 tablespoons fresh orange juice

1. Butter a 13" x 9" shallow baking dish. Mix yeast, 2 tablespoons brown sugar, and ¼ cup warm water in the bowl of a stand mixer; let sit until it foams, about 5 minutes. Whisk in egg and remaining brown sugar, then stir in 1 cup flour and mix with a wooden spoon to incorporate. Sprinkle the remaining 2 cups flour over top but do not mix in. Cover with plastic wrap and let sit in a warm, draft-free spot until mixture is visibly puffed and flour has cracks in places, 1 hour to 1 hour and 30 minutes.

2. Add sour cream, orange zest, orange juice, baking powder, and salt to the mixture and mix on medium speed with a dough hook until smooth, elastic, and just sticking to the sides of the bowl, about 4 minutes. Add 6 tablespoons butter in 2 additions, beating well between additions; beat until a soft, slightly glossy, sticky dough-batter hybrid forms, about 4 minutes.

3. Using buttered fingers, pat dough into a prepared pan in an even layer, spreading to edges. Cover and let sit in a warm, draft-free spot until puffed and nearly doubled in size, 1 hour to 1 hour and 10 minutes.

4. Just before the dough is finished rising, preheat the oven to 350°F. Pulse flour, oats, brown sugar, granulated sugar, cinnamon, and a pinch of salt in a food processor a few times to combine. Add butter and process in long pulses until streusel is the consistency of moist crumbs.

5. Working with several slices at a time, fan out the apples slightly and arrange over dough, shingling rows in different directions; sprinkle streusel over top. Bake until apples are tender and a tester inserted into the center comes out clean, 35 to 45 minutes. Transfer to a wire rack and let cool

6. Whisk powdered sugar, orange juice, and a pinch of salt in a medium bowl, adding more orange juice by the teaspoonful as needed, until the icing is very thick and smooth and falls back onto itself in a slowly dissolving ribbon. Drizzle over coffee cake.

DATE COCONUT ROLLS

An essential for your Rosh Hashanah spread. The New Year prayer typically spoken before eating a date asks that the wicked cease.

YIELD: **12 Servings**

ACTIVE TIME: **30 Minutes**

TOTAL TIME: **2 Hours**

1 cup whole almonds

1 lb. pitted dates

1 cup shredded and chopped coconut (sweetened or unsweetened)

1. In a food processor, combine the almonds and dates and pulse until a paste forms; it is okay is larger chunks of almond remain. Remove the balled up paste from the food processor and roll into 2" logs or balls.

2. Pour the coconut into a shallow dish and then roll and press the date mixture in the coconut. While rolling your hands may become sticky due to the sugar in the dates; rinse your hands with cold water to handle the mixture easily.

3. Refrigerate for at least an hour before serving.

**ROASTED BRUSSELS SPROUTS
WITH WARM HONEY GLAZE**, page 116

YOM KIPPUR

THE IRONY OF TALKING ABOUT Yom Kippur in a cookbook is that the holiest day of the year in the Jewish calendar is more closely associated with fasting, not feasting. It is the Day of Atonement, after all. The center of focus on this holy day is prayer, meditation, or even just quiet reflection, meaning it contrasts sharply with the more lively Rosh Hashanah celebration ten days before. Yom Kippur is one of the most highly observed holidays in Jewish tradition; even many non-practicing Jews will attend synagogue, fast, ask friends and family for forgiveness for any wrongs from the previous year, and work toward self-improvement.

But, even for a day centered on fasting, there's food. Of course there's food.

There are two Yom Kippur meals separated by a 25-hour fast in between. The pre-fast meal is called seudah hamafseket, which translates to "meal of separation" or "concluding meal." Traditionally, one would eat bread, water, and a hard-boiled egg dipped in ashes to commemorate the destruction of the Second Temple and the many other tragedies that have befallen the Jewish people. Over time, however, the meal has expanded to include rice, chicken, or fish. Ashkenazic Jews might eat kreplach or dip challah in honey (a nod back to the Rosh Hashanah celebrations before). For Sephardim, the meal can be festive, but meat and wine are to be avoided. The most important thing to take into consideration when preparing the pre-fast meal is salt; too much sodium can lead to dehydration the next day.

In America and Israel, Ashkenazic traditions call for breaking your fast brunch-style. This is what bagels, lox, and all their delicious accoutrements were made for. Greet your family and loved ones, get your tuchus over to the buffet-style table, and fill up on carbs and dairy in the form of schmear, kugel, quiches, and more. Sephardic tradition is more sweet than savory. One might break their fast with a spoonful of quince preserves or a small, sweet cake, and then finish a savory meal with a honey-soaked pastry or cake. A more traditional meal with soups, stews, or briskets might also be served.

The most important thing is to fill back up while looking forward to a sweet new year and an improved you.

FESENJAN

An Iranian stew that is often flavored with pomegranate paste and ground walnuts and spices like turmeric, cinnamon, orange peel, cardamom, and rosebud. This gorgeous dish traditionally features chicken, but variations with ground meat or lamb also exist.

YIELD: 4 Servings

ACTIVE TIME: 50 Minutes

TOTAL TIME: 1 Hour and 30 Minutes

2 cups shelled walnut halves and pieces

1 tablespoon, plus 1 teaspoon sea salt

2 teaspoons freshly ground black pepper

2 teaspoons cumin

2 teaspoons turmeric

2 lbs. chicken thighs and drumsticks

3 tablespoons avocado oil

1¼ cups Pomegranate Confiture (see recipe)

1 pinch saffron threads (optional)

1. Preheat the oven to 350°F.

2. Spread the walnuts evenly on a rimmed baking sheet and bake until fragrant and toasted, 8 to 10 minutes. Set aside.

3. Place a Dutch oven over medium-high heat for 5 minutes. While the pot is heating, combine the salt, pepper, cumin, and turmeric in a small bowl and mix well. Pat the chicken pieces dry and season with the spice mixture, coating evenly.

4. Add the oil to the pot and swirl to coat. Working in 2 or 3 batches, brown the chicken on all sides, being careful not to overcrowd the pot, about 10 minutes per batch. Transfer the seared chicken to a bowl and repeat with the remaining chicken pieces.

5. Remove the pot from heat and let the oil cool slightly before discarding it. Wipe out any remaining burnt spices and return the pot to the stove.

6. Place the chicken in the pan along with the toasted walnuts, Pomegranate Confiture, and saffron, if using, and stir. Bring to a boil over medium-high heat, then reduce the heat to medium-low, cover with a lid, and simmer for 45 minutes, until the chicken is tender and the walnuts are caramelized.

7. Remove the lid and continue to simmer until the sauce has thickened and the chicken is evenly glazed, 15 to 20 minutes. Remove from the heat and serve immediately.

POMEGRANATE CONFITURE

6 cups pomegranate seeds

3 cups sugar

¼ cup water

1. Place the pomegranate seeds, sugar, and water in a medium saucepan over medium-high heat and bring to a boil. Lower the heat to a simmer and cook until the mixture is thick and syrupy, about 35 minutes. Stir the mixture occasionally to prevent the bottom from burning. Remove from heat and let cool completely before using.

ROASTED BRUSSELS SPROUTS WITH WARM HONEY GLAZE

By preheating the baking sheet, you'll ensure that every sprout in this goes-with-anything side has that irresistible crispy edge. The warm honey glaze adds a sticky sweetness that always seems to pair beautifully with brussels sprouts.

YIELD: **4 Servings**

ACTIVE TIME: **30 Minutes**

TOTAL TIME: **1 Hour**

1½ lbs. brussels sprouts, trimmed and halved

¼ cup avocado oil

½ teaspoon sea salt, plus more to taste

Freshly ground black pepper, to taste

¼ cup honey

⅓ cup sherry vinegar or red wine vinegar

¾ teaspoon crushed red pepper flakes (optional)

3 tablespoons unsalted butter

3 scallions, thinly sliced on a bias

1 teaspoon finely grated lemon zest

1. Place a rack in the bottom third of the oven and set a rimmed baking sheet on top; preheat the oven to 450°F. In a large bowl, combine the brussels sprouts and oil, toss well, and season with salt and pepper, to taste.

2. Carefully remove baking sheet from oven. Using tongs, arrange brussels sprouts, cut-side down, on the hot baking sheet. Roast on the bottom rack until tender and deeply browned, 20 to 25 minutes.

3. Meanwhile, bring honey to a simmer in a small saucepan over medium-high heat. Reduce heat to medium-low and cook, stirring often, until honey is a deep amber color but not burnt (it will be foamy), about 3 minutes. Remove from heat; add vinegar and red pepper flakes, if using, and whisk until sauce is smooth (it will bubble quite aggressively when you first add the vinegar).

4. Set the saucepan over medium heat, add butter and ½ teaspoon salt, and cook, whisking constantly, until glaze is glossy, bubbling, and slightly thickened, about 4 minutes.

5. Transfer brussels sprouts to a large bowl. Add glaze and toss to coat. Transfer to a serving platter and top with scallions and lemon zest.

ROASTED GARLIC POTATO KNISH

So some people serve these as hors d'oeuvres at dinner parties, some still want theirs from a street vendor. Who are we to judge? We're talking about potatoes, garlic, and Schmaltz, baked or fried to perfection here, so you do you.

YIELD: 20 Servings

ACTIVE TIME: 1 Hour

TOTAL TIME: 2 Hours

DOUGH

1 egg, plus 1 for egg wash

½ cup liquid Schmaltz (see page 247), or avocado oil

2 cups all-purpose flour, sifted

½ teaspoon baking powder

½ teaspoon salt

Water as needed

FILLING

5 garlic cloves

¼ cup liquid Schmaltz (see page 247), plus 1 tablespoon and more for drizzling

1 large white onion

½ teaspoon salt

1 lb. russet potatoes

1 bunch scallions, minced

2 eggs

1 teaspoon sea salt

½ teaspoon black pepper

1. Beat egg and Schmaltz, and then add in sifted flour, baking powder, and salt and knead until you have a dough that is not sticky. Add water as needed. Cover and refrigerate for at least an hour.

2. Preheat the oven to 400°F.

3. To start the filling, use a small sheet of tinfoil to roast the garlic by making a packet with garlic cloves and a drizzle of Schmaltz or olive oil. Roast until the garlic is soft, about 40 minutes. Then lower the oven to 375°F.

4. In a skillet, heat 1 tablespoon Schmaltz and caramelize the onions.

5. In a large stockpot, add water, salt, and whole potatoes and bring to a boil; cook until you can stick a knife into the potatoes and it comes out without resistance. Strain water and let potatoes cool enough to handle before peeling and crushing with a fork.

6. In a bowl, mix crushed potatoes with ¼ cup Schmaltz, scallions, roasted garlic, caramelized onions, eggs, 1 teaspoon salt, and ½ teaspoon black pepper.

7. There are many ways to form knishes but we like individual round ones. Roll out your dough until it is as thin as you can get it. Then using a paring knife cut out 6" round discs. Put a ½ cup of filling in each circle and fold in the sides to make a round knish.

8. Place the knishes on baking sheets, brush each one with egg wash, and bake until golden brown, about 25 minutes.

KARTOFFEL KUGEL

There are many variations of potato pudding. This one has a crisp crust and a moist, soft interior. Schmaltz and gribenes add richness and savory flavor, but you can also use vegetable oil and grated carrot if you're going meatless.

YIELD: **6 Servings**

ACTIVE TIME: **30 Minutes**

TOTAL TIME: **1 Hour and 30 Minutes**

½ cup Schmaltz (see page 247) or avocado oil

2 lbs. russet potatoes, peeled

1 cup chopped yellow onions

3 large eggs, lightly beaten

1 teaspoon sea salt

Freshly ground black pepper, to taste

¼ cup Gribenes or grated carrot, optional

⅓ cup matzo meal or all-purpose flour

Crushed matzo, to top

1. Preheat the oven to 375°F. Heat an 8" or 9" square baking dish in the oven.

2. Coat the bottom and sides of the baking dish with ¼ cup of the Schmaltz or oil and return to the oven until very hot, about 15 minutes.

3. Place the potatoes in a large bowl of lightly salted cold water; this keeps them from discoloring.

4. Place the onions into a large bowl and then grate the potatoes into the onions, stirring to mix.

5. Stir in the eggs, remaining ¼ cup schmaltz or oil, salt, pepper, and, if desired, Gribenes or carrot. Add enough matzo meal or flour to bind the batter.

6. Pour into the heated dish, top with crushed matzo, and bake until golden brown, about 1 hour. Although this is best when warm, the leftovers can be served at room temperature.

HONEY-GLAZED CARROTS WITH CARROT TOP GREMOLATA

Dark honeys, like buckwheat, bring a touch of malty sweetness to these lightly glazed beauties. They're perfect for serving with a crispy-skinned roasted chicken. This recipe comes courtesy of Hannah Krieger, aka Honey and Grandma Honey.

YIELD: **8 Servings**

ACTIVE TIME: **15 Minutes**

TOTAL TIME: **30 Minutes**

5 lbs. carrots, with tops

2 garlic cloves, finely chopped

1 tablespoon lemon zest

2 teaspoons extra-virgin olive oil

4 tablespoons unsalted butter

⅓ cup orange juice

1 tablespoon amber honey

1¼ teaspoons sea salt

2 tablespoons fresh lemon juice

⅛ teaspoon cayenne pepper

1. Trim and peel the carrots; reserve the tops. Rinse 1 bunch worth of tops and pat dry. Coarsely chop the carrot tops to make ⅓ cup of carrot tops.

2. In a bowl, combine tops with garlic, lemon zest, oil, and remaining salt and mix well; let stand for at least 20 minutes before using.

3. Add carrots, butter, orange juice, honey, and 1 teaspoon salt to a pot over medium heat, cover, and cook until carrots are tender, about 10 minutes.

4. Uncover carrots and continue to cook, stirring occasionally, until sauce reduces enough to coat carrots, 10 minutes.

5. Remove from heat, stir in lemon juice and cayenne, and season to taste.

6. Transfer carrots to a platter and top with gremolata.

SUMAC AND APPLE-ROASTED CAULIFLOWER, page 141

BAGELS

It doesn't get much better than waking up on a Sunday morning or breaking a long Yom Kippur fast with lox piled high on a bagel. Traditionally, lox is served with cream cheese and garnished with tomato, red onion, cucumbers, and capers.

YIELD: **12 Bagels**

ACTIVE TIME: **1 Hour**

TOTAL TIME: **2 Hours**

1 teaspoon active dry yeast

1¼ cups warm 2% milk (110°F to 115°F)

½ cup unsalted butter, softened

2 tablespoons sugar

1 teaspoon salt

1 egg yolk

3¾–4¼ cups all-purpose flour

Vegetable oil, for greasing

Sesame or poppy seeds (optional)

1. In a large bowl, dissolve the yeast in warm milk. Add the butter, sugar, salt, and egg yolk and mix well. Stir in enough flour to form a soft dough.

2. Turn the dough onto a floured surface and knead until smooth and elastic, 6 to 8 minutes. Place the dough in a greased bowl, turning once to grease the top. Cover and let rise in a warm place until doubled in size, about 1 hour.

3. Punch down the dough and divide into 12 balls. Push thumb through the centers to form a 1½" hole. Stretch and shape the dough to form an even ring. Place on a floured surface, cover, and let rest for 10 minutes, then flatten bagels slightly.

4. Preheat the oven to 400°F. Fill a Dutch oven two-thirds full with water and bring to a boil.

5. Drop the bagels, 2 at a time, into boiling water. Cook for 45 seconds; turn and cook 45 seconds longer. Remove with a slotted spoon drain well on a paper towel-lined plate.

6. Sprinkle with sesame or poppy seeds, if desired. Place the bagels 2" apart on greased baking sheets. Bake until golden brown, about 25 minutes. Let cool on wire racks.

GRANDPA'S GRAVLOX

A tradition to preserve and a recipe to make your zeyde proud. This classic recipe is proof that with a little sugar, salt, and dill, already-delicious and fatty salmon can take on a flavor that you simply can't live without. Grandpa Phil Kramer shared this quintessential Brooklyn-style lox recipe. Make sure to use a very long and very sharp and thin slicing knife when cutting the lox. The thinner the better!

YIELD: 14 Servings

ACTIVE TIME: 1 Hour

TOTAL TIME: 72 Hours

---

1 (3 lb.) salmon fillet, scales removed, skin on

2 cups peeled and grated raw red beets

1¾ cups prepared horseradish

1 large bunch dill, roughly chopped

¾ cup sugar

½ cup coarse sea salt

2 tablespoons cracked black pepper

1. Carefully find any pin bones in the salmon by gently running your hand over the flesh; remove them using needle-nose pliers.

2. Score the skin, making 3 or 4 diagonal, 2 to 3" slashes. Center the fillet, skin-side down, on a large piece of cheesecloth or plastic wrap.

3. In a bowl, combine the remainder of the ingredients, mix well, and pack the mixture in an even layer over the flesh of the salmon; the layer of cure should be slightly thinner where the flesh of the fillet tapers and thins toward the tail.

4. Wrap the salmon loosely in the cheesecloth or plastic wrap and place it in a pan that is large enough to allow the fish to lay flat.

5. Refrigerate the fish for 3 days to allow it to cure. After the third day, gently unwrap the fillet and scrape off the cure. Slice the salmon and serve, or wrap and refrigerate for up to 1 week.

GRANDSON'S BEET & VODKA GRAVLOX

This is the quintessential New York Brooklyn style lox recipe from grandpa jazzed up because grandson was a big shot New York chef! Kids these days. Tradition or not, beet and vodka enhance this classic recipe, giving it a zing that even Bubbe can't argue with.

Still, make sure to use a very long and very sharp, thin slicing knife when cutting the lox. The thinner the better! And be sure to treat yourself to a shot of vodka and a taste of caviar as you prepare the salmon.

YIELD: **14 Servings**

ACTIVE TIME: **1 Hour**

TOTAL TIME: **72 Hours**

---

1 (3 lb.) salmon fillet, scales removed and skin on

2 cups peeled and grated raw red beets

¾ cup prepared horseradish

1 cup vodka

1 large bunch dill, roughly chopped

1 large bunch cilantro, stems and leaves

¾ cup sugar

½ cup coarse sea salt

2 tablespoons cracked black pepper

1 tablespoon sumac

Zest of 1 lemon

Toast points, for serving

1 oz. golden Osetra caviar, to serve

Crème fraîche, for serving

Fresh dill sprigs, for serving

1. Carefully find any pin bones in the salmon by gently running your hand over the flesh; remove them using needle-nose pliers.

2. Score the skin, making 3 or 4 diagonal, 2 to 3" slashes. Center the fillet, skin-side down, on a large piece of cheesecloth or plastic wrap.

3. In a bowl, combine the cure ingredients, mix well, and pack the mixture in an even layer over the flesh of the salmon; the layer of cure should be slightly thinner where the flesh of the fillet tapers and thins toward the tail.

4. Wrap the salmon loosely in the cheesecloth or plastic wrap and place it in a pan that is large enough to allow the fish to lay flat.

5. Refrigerate the fish for 3 days to allow it to cure. After the third day, gently unwrap the fillet and scrape off the cure. Slice the salmon and serve, or wrap and refrigerate for up to 1 week.

6. Serve lox on toast points with caviar, crème fraîche, and dill sprigs.

**TURKISH EGGPLANT
SALAD**, page 140

MATJES HERRING IN RED WINE SAUCE OR CREAM SAUCE

This herring can be served raw in vinegar or baked in its marinade and then served cold. Never for the faint of heart, its strong, pungent flavor is only enhanced when served with cut onions.

YIELD: **4 Servings**

ACTIVE TIME: **20 Minutes**

TOTAL TIME: **74 Hours**

½ cup white wine vinegar

½ cup red wine vinegar

1 cup sugar

1½ cups water

1½ oz. carrots, finely chopped

4 white sweet onions, thinly sliced

1½ oz. celery root, grated

2 teaspoons mashed garlic cloves

3 teaspoons allspice

2 cinnamon sticks, crushed

5 bay leaves

5 white peppercorns

5 black peppercorns

15 coriander seeds, toasted

2 teaspoons Nigella seeds

1 small piece of horseradish, peeled

5 salted herring fillets

CREAM SAUCE

3 cups full-fat sour cream

1 cup heavy cream

¼ cup sugar

1 teaspoon sumac

2 teaspoons grated horseradish

1 teaspoon fresh cracked coarse black pepper

1 teaspoon chopped dill

½ teaspoon cumin

¼ teaspoon sea salt

1. In a pot, combine all of the ingredients, except the herring, bring to a boil, and then remove from heat and let cool.

2. As the stock is being prepared soak the herring in ice water for 3 hours.

3. Add the herring to the stock and refrigerate for 3 days; make sure to stir the marinating fish once per day.

4. Remove the herring from the marinade, slice into bite-sized pieces, and place in a serving bowl.

5. Sieve out and discard the bay leaves and most (but not all) of the pickling spices from the stock, keeping the onions and the marinade with the fish.

6. Finally, if using, add Cream Sauce, combine well, and serve cold.

Cream Sauce

1. In a bowl, combine all of the ingredients and mix well.

RED CABBAGE, DATE & BEET SALAD

This salad is a beautiful burst of deep reds and savory-sweet ingredients.

YIELD: 6 Servings

ACTIVE TIME: 30 Minutes

TOTAL TIME: 1 Hour and 30 Minutes

---

2 cups kosher salt

6 large red beets

½ head red cabbage, cored and thinly sliced crosswise

5 dried medjool dates, pitted and thinly sliced lengthwise

½ cup tahini

⅓ cup finely chopped cilantro

⅓ cup finely chopped mint

⅓ cup finely chopped scallions

1 teaspoon sea salt

¼ cup extra-virgin olive oil

¼ cup fresh lemon juice

1. Preheat the oven to 395°F. Line a baking sheet with parchment paper and cover with kosher salt.

2. Place the beets on the bed of kosher salt and bake for about 40 minutes, until fork-tender. Let the beets cool for 30 minutes and then peel them, discarding the peels and salt.

3. Julienne the beets, cutting them into 2" slices that are ⅛" thick or use a grater and grate the beets into a bowl.

4. Add all of the remaining ingredients to the beets, mix well, and season to taste. Serve immediately.

PICKLED CUCUMBER SALAD

Pickles and other pickled veggies play a big part in Jewish cuisine. This salad in particular marries those traditional flavors in a dish with lots of squeaky bite.

YIELD: **8 Servings**
ACTIVE TIME: **10 Minutes**
TOTAL TIME: **25 Minutes**

1 teaspoon sugar

¼ cup rice vinegar

2 large cucumbers, peeled and thinly sliced crosswise

½ medium red onion, thinly sliced

Sea salt, to taste

Freshly ground black pepper

1 tablespoon chopped curly-leaf parsley

1. In a large bowl, combine the sugar and vinegar and whisk until the sugar is dissolved.

2. Place the cucumber and onion slices in the marinade for at least 15 minutes.

3. Sprinkle with salt, pepper, and parsley and serve.

PICKLED GREEN TOMATOES

We're not saying you can't eat a pastrami sandwich without these, but why would you want to? Squeaky, soft, sweet, and acidic, each bite of pickled green tomatoes is a burst of different sensations.

YIELD: **2 Pints**

ACTIVE TIME: **15 Minutes**

TOTAL TIME: **1 Week**

1½ cups distilled white vinegar or apple-cider vinegar

¾ cup water

2 teaspoons sugar

½ teaspoon whole black peppercorns

½ teaspoon coriander seeds

½ teaspoon caraway seeds

½ teaspoon cumin seeds

3 whole allspice berries

2 dried bay leaves

2 tablespoons coarse sea salt

1 lb. small green tomatoes, cut into ¼" slices

6 thin slices white onion

1. Combine vinegar, water, sugar, spices, and salt in a saucepan. Bring to a boil, stirring until sugar is dissolved.

2. Fill clean containers tightly with tomatoes and onion.

3. Add boiling brine to cover completely. Let cool completely.

4. Cover, label, and refrigerate at least 1 week before serving, or up to 3 months.

LABNEH

Congratulations, you're about to pull off the easiest recipe for homemade cheese! This is a strained yogurt cheese, dried and prepared either as a buttery spread or shaped into balls. Native to the Middle East, labneh cheese is a popular food in Israel. Creamy labneh is usually spread out onto a pita bread or a bagel, and blends well with lemon juice, olive oil, za'atar, and herbs like marjoram, oregano, thyme, and sesame seeds.

YIELD: **2½ Cups**

ACTIVE TIME: **10 Minutes**

TOTAL TIME: **25 to 48 Hours**

32 oz. whole cow's milk yogurt or Greek yogurt

½ teaspoon salt

1 tablespoon olive oil, for serving

1-2 teaspoons Za'atar (see page 248)

1. Add the yogurt to a large bowl and season it with the salt; the salt helps pull out excess whey, giving you a creamier, thicker cheese.

2. Place a fine-mesh strainer on top of a medium-sized bowl. Line the strainer with cheesecloth or a linen kitchen towel, letting a few inches hang over the side of the strainer. Spoon the seasoned yogurt into the cheesecloth and gently wrap the sides over the top of the yogurt, protecting it from being exposed to air in the refrigerator.

3. Store everything in the refrigerator for 24 to 48 hours, discarding the whey halfway through if the bowl beneath the strainer becomes too full.

4. Remove the labneh from the cheesecloth and store it in an airtight container.

5. To serve as a dip, press a dent in the center of the cheese, drizzling the olive oil into the center and sprinkling it with Za'atar.

TURKISH EGGPLANT SALAD

At its core, our food is Turkish in one form or another. My grandmother was Turkish through and through, and my father's food bears the same fingerprints. Our eggplant salad is more than likely the purest show of our Turkish heritage: unmistakably garlic heavy, smoky, earthy.

YIELD: **4 Servings**

ACTIVE TIME: **30 Minutes**

TOTAL TIME: **1 Hour and 30 Minutes**

2 large eggplants

2 tablespoons olive oil

3 medium tomatoes, large dice

1 white onion, julienned

4 garlic cloves

1 tablespoon paprika

1 teaspoon kosher salt

1 teaspoon cumin

1 teaspoon cayenne

½ cup chopped parsley

1. In either a 450°F oven or on a grill set to high, char eggplants until they are fully softened and somewhat shriveled; this not an exact science, but longer is better, 40 minutes to 1 hour. Allow to cool.

2. Add the oil to a large frying pan over high heat. When the oil begins to shimmer add the tomatoes and onions, followed by the remainder of the ingredients, except the parsley. Cook for approximately 20 minutes, stirring occasionally. Remove from heat.

3. Split open the eggplants and scoop out the soft flesh and fold it into the tomato mixture, adding the parsley as you go. Serve at room temperature.

SUMAC & APPLE-ROASTED CAULIFLOWER

Whole roasted cauliflower is a staple of the modern Israeli kitchen. By roasting the cauliflower covered it gets very soft while also absorbing the onion, apple, and sumac flavors. This soft but crispy version is sweet and creamy.

YIELD: **4 Servings**

ACTIVE TIME: **20 Minutes**

TOTAL TIME: **1 Hour and 15 Minutes**

1 apple, peeled and quartered

1 onion, quartered

1 tablespoon sumac

1 tablespoon kosher salt

1 tablespoon sugar

½ cup water

1 whole cauliflower

2 tablespoons honey

2 tablespoons tahini

1. Preheat the oven to 400°F.

2. Combine the apple, onion, sumac, salt, sugar, and water in a food processor and pulse.

3. Using a sharp knife, remove any leaves from the cauliflower and square off the stem. Place the cauliflower head in a roasting pan and coat with the apple and onion mixture. Wrap with foil and roast for 45 minutes, until the cauliflower is soft enough to cut into with a fork. Set the oven to 450°F and finish the cauliflower for 10 more minutes uncovered.

4. To serve, set the cauliflower on a rimmed plate and drizzle with honey and tahini.

SHAVED SNAP PEA SALAD

This salad depends on the thin slicing of the snap peas and the quality of the honey to fully blossom into the beautiful salad it is meant to be. At its best, this is a vibrant mix of sweet and acidic, herby and crunchy.

YIELD: **2 Servings**

ACTIVE TIME: **30 Minutes**

TOTAL TIME: **1 Hour**

1 lb. snap peas

1 tablespoon chopped dill

1 tablespoon chopped basil

1 tablespoon chopped mint

2 teaspoons honey

¼ cup white vinegar

1 teaspoon kosher salt

1 tablespoon crushed toasted walnuts

1. Using a sharp knife, stack 4 snap peas at a time and cut thin slices on the bias. Once all of the snap peas are cut, put them into a medium-sized bowl.

2. By hand, mix all of the other ingredients into the peas, making sure to thoroughly incorporate them all.

3. Allow the salad to stand for at least 30 minutes, and up to an hour, before serving.

PASSOVER

PASSOVER IS THE MAJOR Jewish spring festival that lasts seven or eight days, starting on the 15th day of Nisan, or mid-March to April on the Gregorian calendar. This incredibly important holiday commemorates the liberation of the Israelites from Egyptian slavery. Perhaps more than any other festivity on the Jewish calendar, Passover is about history, tradition, and community. These elements are tied in to nearly every holiday, but Passover in particular is a reminder of the hardships that the Jewish people have faced from the time of Pharoah onward. Celebration is in order, of course, but at the heart of Passover is a remembrance of the bitterness of oppression—and gratitude for deliverance, fortitude, and resilience.

Yom Kippur is considered the holiest of holidays, but it is almost without question that Passover is the most culturally defining.

Memory and emotion are evoked at the seder. Much of the food eaten is deeply symbolic. Not only is this when matzo is served to represent the unleavened bread that Jews ate while fleeing Egypt, but all leavened bread (and desserts) should be abstained from throughout.

Horseradish is eaten as a reminder of the bitterness of slavery, while haroset—a mixture of apples, nuts, and wine—symbolizes the mortar the Jewish people used to construct pyramids, temples, and other buildings in Egypt.

For Sephardim and Ashkenazim, the Passover meal can feature lamb at the center. Not only is lamb in keeping with spring—the "lambing" season—but this meat in particular is symbolic of the paschal sacrifice. The main course can also be brisket. Sephardic Passover will then have a plethora of colorful side dishes, such as jeweled rice, crunchy salads, and other savory-sweet vegetables.

Ashkenazi Jews celebrate eating matzo in a variety of ways. Machine-made matzo wasn't common until the 19th century; before that, people would buy matzo from their bakeries and use the crumbs for matzo balls. So matzo ball soup is always welcome at a Passover meal, as well as matzo lasagna or even matzo icebox cake. Other desserts, such as macaroons and flourless chocolate cake are ideal treats for a leaven-free celebration.

RED GEFILTE FISH VERACRUZANA

If you're thinking of the white-fish spread, think again. This patty of white fish, vegetables, and matzo meal is cooked in a rich tomato sauce—the perfect bite for a Jewish Chilanga Passover.

YIELD: **10 Servings**

ACTIVE TIME: **30 Minutes**

TOTAL TIME: **2 Hours**

FISH BROTH

1 teaspoon caraway seeds

1 teaspoon fennel seeds

1 teaspoon cumin seeds

1 teaspoon coriander seeds

1 star anise

1 cinnamon stick

5 bay leaves

1 bunch parsley stems

3 medium carrots, sliced into rounds

3 celery ribs

3 white sweet onions, sliced thin

Fish bones and heads from snapper and pike

1 gallon water

1 cup white wine

1 cup red wine

1 orange peel

1 lemon, halved

FISH MIXTURE

4 lbs. ground pike

2 lbs. ground red snapper

2 large carrots, peeled and grated

½ large onion, peeled and grated

4 large eggs

¾ cup matzo meal

1½ tablespoons fine sea salt

1½ teaspoons white pepper

VERACRUZANA SAUCE

2 tablespoons olive oil

4 whole garlic cloves, peeled

1 cup Texas onions, sliced thin on bias

¼ cup sliced shallots

2 garlic cloves finely minced

6-8 oz. jar capers

8-10 oz. can green olives, cut in half

4 cups tomatoes diced

1/3 cup parsley

2 bay leaves

⅛ teaspoon cinnamon

¼ teaspoon dried oregano

2 cups Fish Broth from above, with sliced carrots and thinly sliced onions

Salt and pepper, to taste

1. Place all of the broth ingredients in an 8- to 10-quart stockpot, bring to a boil, lower heat, cover, and simmer for 15 minutes.

2. Remove from heat and then remove the bones from the broth, keeping the broth hot on low heat, while you make the fish mixture.

3. Place all of the ground fish, grated carrots, and onions in a large bowl and mix. Add matzo meal, eggs, salt, and pepper and with hand mix gently but thoroughly, until fish is light in texture and holds its shape.

4. Using damp hands, take about ⅓-½ cup quantities of the fish mixture, shape into oval patties, and gently drop into the broth, which is hot but not boiling. When you have dropped the last fish patty into the broth, raise the heat and simmer for 1 hour.

5. As the gefilte fish cooks, start the sauce by adding oil to a large saucepan over medium-high heat. Add the 4 garlic cloves and sauté for a few minutes, removing them from the oil when they begin to turn golden. Add the onions and shallots and stir until translucent then add back the roasted garlic cloves and fry the capers and the green olives, mix for 2 minutes, and then add the diced tomatoes. Stir and then allow to simmer for 5 minutes. Add the parsley, bay leaves, oregano, cinnamon, and fish stock with carrots and onions. Season with salt and pepper to taste, and simmer for 10 more minutes.

6. After the fish has simmered for 1 hour in the broth, transfer the fish loaves to the pan containing the sauce. Simmer the fish in the sauce for 10 minutes and then remove from heat. Arrange the fish on a serving platter and cover with the sauce from the pan. Garnish with all the vegetables from the sauce and serve warm or hot.

MATZO BREI, page 150

MATZO BREI

Matzo Brei is eaten during Passover, when leavened bread is strictly forbidden. This recipe, which calls for dry matzo to be broken into pieces, softened in water or milk, mixed with eggs, and fried, is a great substitute for those who enjoy eggs and toast for breakfast.

YIELD: **2 Servings**

ACTIVE TIME: **10 Minutes**

TOTAL TIME: **20 Minutes**

6 sheets of matzo

Boiling water

4 eggs

Sea salt, to taste

White pepper, to taste

1 tablespoon avocado oil

1. In a large bowl, break matzo into fragments. Not too small! Sprinkle with a little boiling water—no more than ¼ cup.

2. While matzo is softening, beat the eggs. Pour over softened matzo, add salt and pepper, and mix well.

3. Add oil to a frying pan over medium heat. When the oil is hot, add the matzo mixture, stirring until the brei is dry but not crisp, about 7 to 10 minutes.

4. Serve with cinnamon and sugar, honey, or preserves (blackberry jam is particularly good). Matzo brei cools quickly. It can be reheated in the microwave.

OLIVE SALAD

A starter with Persian roots also popularized in Jewish Chilanga cuisine. This cold salad is made ahead by combining green olives, garlic, and pomegranate.

YIELD: **6 Servings**

ACTIVE TIME: **15 Minutes**

TOTAL TIME: **15 Minutes**

2 cups pitted green olives

2 garlic cloves, finely chopped

1 cup pomegranate seeds

⅓ cup pomegranate concentrate

⅓ cup plus 1 tablespoon roughly chopped mint, divided

⅓ cup olive oil

1 teaspoon sea salt

¼ teaspoon ground black pepper

1 teaspoon roughly crushed roasted walnuts, for garnish

1. In a bowl, combine the olives, garlic, and pomegranate seeds and mix well.

2. In another bowl, add the pomegranate concentrate, ⅓ cup mint, and olive oil and mix until combined into a dressing. Pour the dressing over the olive mixture and stir well, until evenly coated. Add salt and pepper and mix well. Place the salad into an airtight container and refrigerate until serving.

3. Transfer the salad into a serving bowl and garnish with walnuts and remaining tablespoon of mint.

CHAROSET

This sweet apple-wine-nut mixture is eaten on Passover not just for its sweetness but to represent the mortar the slaves used in building the pyramids.

YIELD: **6 Servings**

ACTIVE TIME: **15 Minutes**

TOTAL TIME: **1 Hour and 15 Minutes**

1/2 cup finely chopped walnuts

3 medium Gala or Fuji apples, peeled and finely chopped

2 tablespoons sweet red wine or grape juice

2 tablespoons sugar

1 teaspoon ground cinnamon

Matzo (optional)

1. Place the walnuts in a skillet over low heat and cook until lightly browned, stirring occasionally.

2. In a large bowl, toss apples and walnuts with wine.

3. In a small bowl, mix the sugar and cinnamon and then sprinkle over apple mixture and toss to combine.

4. Refrigerate, covered, for 1 hour before serving. If desired, serve with matzo.

ROMANO BEANS WITH MUSTARD VINAIGRETTE & WALNUTS

Romano beans, also known as Italian pole beans, are wide and flat and have a less delicate texture than green beans but share their mild, sweet flavor.

YIELD: **8 Servings**

ACTIVE TIME: **15 Minutes**

TOTAL TIME: **1 Hour**

---

1 cup walnuts

3 lbs. Romano beans or green beans, trimmed

3 tablespoons red wine vinegar

2 tablespoons Dijon mustard

1 garlic clove, finely grated

2 tablespoons extra-virgin olive oil, plus more for drizzling

Zest of ½ lemon

¾ cup very coarsely chopped parsley

Freshly ground black pepper, to taste

1. Preheat the oven to 350°F.

2. Toast walnuts on a rimmed baking sheet, tossing once, until golden brown, 8 to 10 minutes. Let cool, then coarsely chop.

3. Cook the beans in a large pot of boiling salted water until bright green and tender, 8 to 10 minutes. Using a slotted spoon, transfer to a bowl of ice water and let cool. Drain and pat dry.

4. Meanwhile, in a large bowl, combine the vinegar, mustard, garlic, and 2 tablespoons oil and mix well. Let sit for 10 minutes for flavors to come together.

5. Add walnuts and beans to dressing. Finely zest lemon over beans and add parsley. Season with salt and lots of pepper and toss to coat. Transfer to a platter and drizzle with more oil.

TZIMMES CHICKEN WITH APRICOTS, PRUNES & CARROTS, page 162

GEFILTE FISH

Gefilte fish is one of those foods that your cousin dares you to try every year on Passover. Although opinions vary on this traditional Jewish food, white fish lovers can rejoice while noshing on this appetizer. In the Torah, it uses the word "blessing" three times with the first regarding the creation of fish. When a person eats fish on Shabbat, he or she is the beneficiary of a triple blessing. This recipe has been provided by Nana Tillie and Grandma Fannie.

YIELD: **12 to 16 pieces**

ACTIVE TIME: **30 Minutes**

TOTAL TIME: **1 Hour and 30 Minutes**

COOKING BROTH

4 quarts water

2½ cups dry white wine

1 medium onion, thinly sliced

1 medium carrot, peeled and sliced into rounds

½ lemon, cut into slices

2 bay leaves

2 tablespoons sea salt

½ bunch fresh thyme

½ bunch fresh flat leaf parsley

¼ teaspoon whole black peppercorns

¼ teaspoon whole fennel seeds

FISH

1 lb. skinless filleted cod, diced into small ½" pieces

1 lb. skinless filleted white fish, diced into small ½" pieces

1 lb. skinless filleted pike, diced into small ½" pieces

1 cup grated onion

½ cup grated carrot

½ cup grated celery

1 lemon, zested

1 tablespoon minced fennel fronds

3 extra-large eggs

½ cup heavy cream

2 tablespoons sugar

1 teaspoon garlic powder

1 tablespoon sea salt

1½ teaspoons fresh ground black pepper

½ cup matzo meal

¼ cup cold water

1. In a large stockpot, combine water, wine, onion, carrot, lemon, bay leaves, and salt. Create an herb pouch with the thyme, parsley, peppercorns and fennel seeds and add to the pot. Cover the pot and bring to a simmer over medium-low heat for 30 minutes. Discard herb pouch. Remove 1 quart of broth and chill for later to cool cooked fish. Set aside the remainder of the broth.

2. Place fish and all remaining ingredients, except matzo meal and water, in a food processor and puree until smooth, about 2 to 3 minutes. When the mixture is well combined and smooth, transfer to a chilled bowl and add matzo meal hydrated by the water to create a binder. Mix until thoroughly incorporated and refrigerate for 1 hour.

3. In a separate bowl, fill with ice water and wet your hands in the water as you roughly shape 4 oz. portions of the fish mixture into ovals. Refrigerate the raw fish once formed.

4. Bring the cooking broth to a gentle simmer.

5. Working in batches, add one layer of the gefilte fish to the pot and poach until the fish turns opaque and its shape is set, about 5 minutes. Using a slotted spoon turn the fish over and continue to cook, until the fish is fully poached, about 12 to 15 minutes. Using a thermometer, check the temperature of the fish, it should read 135°F.

6. Remove the gefilte fish from the poaching liquid and transfer to a cold bowl, allowing the gefilte fish to cool in the cold reserved broth from earlier. Place the whole bowl on top of another bowl of ice for about 20 minutes until completely chilled. Place cooked fish in the refrigerator overnight before serving.

   TIP: Keep all of the fish in a bowl in ice. The colder the fish is the better it will be to make the force meat.

RUSTIC MATZO BALL SOUP

This recipe has been shared by Lynn Krieger Gilden, lovingly known as Mom, Minama, and Grandma Lynn.

YIELD: **12 Servings**

ACTIVE TIME: **30 Minutes**

TOTAL TIME: **2 Hours**

SOUP

1 (4 lb.) whole chicken

2 lbs. chicken legs

2 lbs. chicken thighs

1 (14½ oz.) can chicken stock

1¾ teaspoons sea salt, divided

1 lb. carrots, chopped

½ lb. parsnip, chopped

6 celery ribs, chopped

3 medium sweet onions, chopped

1 garlic clove, minced

¼ teaspoon black pepper

¼ cup minced parsley

¼ teaspoon celery salt

¼ teaspoon onion powder

MATZO BALLS

4 eggs

5 tablespoons unsalted butter

1½ tablespoons Schmaltz (see page 247)

⅓ cup water

12 oz. matzo meal

¼ cup diced onion,

1 tablespoon garlic powder

1 teaspoon onion powder

1 teaspoon sea salt

1 teaspoon black pepper

1. Place chicken in a large stockpot, add the stock, 1 teaspoon salt, and enough water to cover the chicken. Bring to a boil. Reduce heat and simmer until there is no more need for skimming the surface as foam rises.

2. Add the remainder of the ingredients and bring to a boil, then reduce heat and simmer for 1 hour and 30 minutes.

3. When done remove the chicken and set aside.

4. Add some of the contents of the pot to a food processor and puree. Place the puree into a clean pot and repeat until three-quarters of the pot is blended. Reserve the leftover carrots, onions, and celery to add to each soup bowl.

5. In a small bowl, whisk eggs and oil. Add the remainder of the ingredients and mix with a fork until combined. Cover and refrigerate for 15 minutes.

6. Remove and discard skin and bones from chicken; chop chicken and add to the blended soup. Stir in parsley, bring to a boil.

7. Using a teaspoon and wet hands, scoop 12 rounded matzo balls and gently add to the boiling soup.

8. Reduce heat, cover, and simmer for 25 minutes, or until a toothpick inserted into a matzo ball comes out clean; do not lift cover while simmering.

9. With a slotted spoon, carefully remove matzo balls and place 2 or 3 in each soup bowl.

TZIMMES CHICKEN WITH APRICOTS, PRUNES & CARROTS

This holiday-ready dinner has all the flavors of tzimmes, the traditional side dish made with stewed dried fruits and honey. Roasted on baking sheets with colorful young carrots, it feeds a crowd with minimal effort.

YIELD: **8 Servings**

ACTIVE TIME: **50 Minutes**

TOTAL TIME: **1 Hour and 40 Minutes**

2 (4 lb.) whole chicken, broken down into 8 pieces, wings and backbones reserved for another use

4 teaspoons sea salt, divided

½ cup plus 2 tablespoons honey

½ cup avocado oil

½ cup fresh lemon juice

2 teaspoons freshly ground black pepper

2 teaspoons cinnamon

1 teaspoon cumin

¼ teaspoon cayenne pepper

2 lbs. carrots, preferably young carrots with greens attached, halved lengthwise

1 large red onion, cut into ½" wedges

12 garlic cloves, peeled

8 oz. dried apricots

8 oz. dried prunes

20 sprigs fresh thyme

1½ cups dry white wine

Parsley leaves with tender stems, for serving (optional)

1. Arrange racks in the top and lower thirds of the oven and preheat it to 400°F.

2. Season chicken pieces with 2 teaspoons salt.

3. In a large bowl, combine the honey, oil, lemon juice, pepper, cinnamon, cumin, cayenne, and remaining 2 teaspoons salt and whisk well. Add chicken pieces, carrots, onion, garlic, apricots, prunes, and thyme and toss to combine.

4. Divide everything, except the chicken, between 2 rimmed baking sheets.

5. In a measuring cup, combine the wine with ½ cup water, then pour half over each sheet.

6. Cover sheets tightly with foil and roast for 15 minutes, then remove from the oven. Remove foil, divide chicken between sheets, and continue to roast, rotating sheets top to bottom halfway through, until carrots are fork-tender, chicken is golden brown, and an instant-read thermometer inserted into the thickest part of a breast registers 165°F, 30 to 35 minutes (if some pieces of chicken are finished before others, transfer them to a serving platter).

7. Transfer chicken mixture to a serving platter. Pour pan juices over. If desired, top with parsley before serving.

CHOPPED LIVER

We know, we know, chopped liver often gets a bad rap. But try this recipe shared by Beth Krieger, aka Aunite Beth, and realize why this mainstay has withstood the test of time and deserves a lot more love.

YIELD: **20 servings**

ACTIVE TIME: **25 Minutes**

TOTAL TIME: **1 Hour and 10 Minutes**

1½ lbs. chicken livers

¼ cup Schmaltz (see page 247), divided

Sea salt, to taste

Freshly ground black pepper, to taste

4 large sweet onions, sliced

5 hard-boiled eggs, diced

½ cup Gribenes, plus more to garnish

2 tablespoons minced parsley, to garnish

1. Prepare the livers by cutting off any tough or stringy pieces.

2. Add 2 teaspoons Schmaltz to a large skillet over medium heat. Put half of the chicken livers into the skillet and fry them for 4 minutes on each side. Season the livers generously with salt and pepper as they are cooking. The livers should be cooked to medium, meaning firm and browned on the outside while slightly pink on the inside. Do not overcook the livers!

3. When the livers are done, pour them into a medium-size bowl along with the leftover Schmaltz from the pan.

4. Add another 2 teaspoons Schmaltz to the skillet, and repeat the process until all of the livers are cooked.

5. Add the onions to the skillet and reduce heat to medium-low. Cover the skillet and cook for about 10 minutes. Uncover the skillet, stir the onions, and continue to sauté them for another 30 minutes.

6. Add the cooked onions to the mixing bowl along with 4 of the diced hard-boiled eggs and the Gribenes. Season with salt and pepper.

7. Place all of the ingredients in a food processor and pulse in 20-second intervals until a roughly textured paste forms. Season to taste with salt and pepper.

8. Refrigerate the chopped liver until ready to serve. Garnish with the remaining egg, Gribenes, and parsley.

FAVA BEANS WITH POMEGRANATES

Spring in a dish with these young fava beans and plenty of fresh herbs.

YIELD: **4 Servings**

ACTIVE TIME: **20 Minutes**

TOTAL TIME: **30 Minutes**

½ red onion, thinly sliced

1 teaspoon sumac

1 teaspoon red wine vinegar

½ teaspoon sea salt,
plus more to taste

2 tablespoons avocado oil

2 garlic cloves, chopped

1½ lbs. fresh young fava beans,
pod and inner shell removed

¼ teaspoon black pepper

1 teaspoon Za'atar
(see page 248)

Juice of ½ lemon

½ cup fresh parsley

¼ cup fresh dill

¼ cup fresh mint

¼ cup pomegranate seeds

1 teaspoon pomegranate
molasses

2 tablespoons extra virgin
olive oil

2 tablespoons Labneh
(see page 139)

1. In a bowl, combine the onions with sumac and red wine vinegar and a pinch of sea salt. Allow to sit for 10 minutes. The onions will turn bright red and become slightly pickled.

2. Add avocado oil to a large saucepan over medium-low heat and sauté the garlic and fava beans until the beans become bright green in color. Season with sea salt, pepper, Za'atar, and lemon juice.

3. Remove from heat and add fresh herbs and pomegranates and garnish with onions, pomegranate molasses, extra virgin olive oil, and Labneh.

JEWISH-STYLE FRIED ARTICHOKES

Carciofi alla giudìa, or Jewish-style artichokes, originated in the Jewish-Roman ghetto of Rome and are still popular in Jewish-Roman restaurants during the spring when artichokes are in season. The artichokes are seasoned with lemon juice, salt, and pepper, and then deep fried in olive oil. The finishing touch is the sprinkling of a little cold water on the artichokes for added crispness, resulting in a golden sunflower, its leaves crunching with every bite.

YIELD: **8 Servings**
ACTIVE TIME: **1 Hour and 15 Minutes**
TOTAL TIME: **2 Hours**

5 lemons

4 large artichokes

Avocado oil, for frying

Salt and pepper, to taste

1. Prepare a large bowl of ice water. Squeeze two lemons into the bowl of water, stir, then throw in the squeezed lemon halves. This lemon water will keep the artichokes fresh and green until you're ready to fry them. Keep a couple of fresh lemon halves on hand as you prep.

2. Rinse the artichokes under cold water. Pat them dry with a clean kitchen towel or paper towel. With kitchen shears or sharp scissors, remove the thorny tips from the leaves. For each artichoke, remove the bitter, fibrous end of the stem with a knife, leaving about 1½" of stem attached to the artichoke.

3. Use a serrated knife to peel the outer skin from the remaining stem. The stem has a more bitter taste than the rest of the artichoke; removing the skin helps to take away some of the bitterness. Rub the peeled stem with fresh lemon to keep it from browning.

4. Peel off 5 to 6 layers of external leaves from the artichoke, snapping off the leaves and setting them aside, until you reach inner leaves that are fresh looking and white at the base.

5. With a serrated knife or sharp chef's knife, slice the artichoke horizontally, about ¾" above the base (heart), to remove the pointy top of the artichoke, leaving a flat crown of leaves on the base of the artichoke while exposing the inner purple leaves.

6. Slice the artichoke in half lengthwise, splitting the stem and heart in half vertically to reveal the inner fuzzy choke.

7. Scoop out the fuzzy white spines and purple leaves from each artichoke half with a melon baller, leaving behind two hollowed out halves of heart, each with a small crown of flat leaves.

8. Rub the heart with lemon, then place it in the bowl of lemon water. Repeat the process with the remaining artichokes.

9. When ready to cook, remove the artichoke halves from the lemon water. Pour the lemon water and juiced lemon halves into a large pot; you will need about 1½" of water, so if you don't have enough, add more water to top it off. Place a steamer basket inside the pot and bring water to a boil. Place the cleaned artichoke halves in the steamer basket and cover the pot with a lid. Reduce heat to medium.

10. Let the artichokes steam for 15 to 20 minutes, until a knife or fork can be inserted easily into the thickest part of the stem. You want the artichokes to be lightly steamed and a bit tender, but still firm—they should only be partially cooked.

11. Place the steamed artichoke halves onto a layer of paper towels and let them drain and dry completely before frying.

12. Heat 1" of oil to 325°F, hot enough for frying but not so hot that it smokes. While the oil is heating, sprinkle the artichoke halves with salt and pepper, making sure to sprinkle inside the layers of leaves as well.

13. Gently place the artichokes into the heated oil and let them fry for about 15 minutes, using a pair of tongs to turn them once halfway through cooking, until the artichokes are golden brown and the leaves are crisp.

14. Remove from the oil and let them drain on paper towels or a wire rack.

15. Serve warm with fresh sliced lemon wedges.

TIP: Use a serrated bread knife to peel and cut the outer leaves and stems of the artichokes as the knife's teeth will cut easier. These artichokes are great with Chermoula.

**LEG OF LAMB WITH
GARLIC & ROSEMARY,**
page 170

LEG OF LAMB WITH GARLIC & ROSEMARY

A classic recipe to recreate, and pass on, year after year. This beautifully seasoned leg of lamb is the star of any Passover table.

YIELD: **8 Servings**

ACTIVE TIME: **30 Minutes**

TOTAL TIME: **2 Hours and 30 Minutes**

1 (7 lb.) semi-boneless leg of lamb, fat trimmed to ¼" thick, and lamb tied

4 garlic cloves

1 tablespoon fine sea salt

2 tablespoons chopped fresh rosemary

2 tablespoons Ras el Hanout

2 tablespoons sumac

2 tablespoons Berbere Spice Mix (see page 248)

½ teaspoon black pepper

¼ cup dry red wine or Beef Stock (see page 246)

1. Pat the lamb dry and score fat by making shallow cuts all over with the tip of a sharp, small knife.

2. Using a mortar and pestle, pound the garlic to a paste with sea salt and stir together with rosemary, all of the spices, and pepper. Put lamb in a lightly oiled roasting pan, then rub paste all over lamb. Let stand at room temperature for 30 minutes.

3. Preheat the oven to 350°F.

4. Roast the lamb in the middle of the oven until an instant-read thermometer inserted 2" into the thickest part of meat registers 130°F, 1½ to 1¾ hours. Transfer to a cutting board and let stand 15 to 25 minutes (internal temperature will rise to about 135°F for medium-rare).

5. Add wine to pan and deglaze by boiling over moderately high heat, stirring and scraping up brown bits, about 1 minute. Season pan juices with salt and pepper and serve with lamb.

ROSEMARY RACK OF LAMB WITH ROASTED POTATOES & CARROTS

This elegant dinner of lamb, miso butter–basted potatoes, and honey-glazed carrots is the perfect size for a small, intimate dinner party. But only make if you're prepared to be everyone's favorite new chef.

YIELD: **2 Servings**

ACTIVE TIME: **30 Minutes**

TOTAL TIME: **1 Hour and 30 Minutes**

---

1 (1-1½ lb.) rack of lamb, fat cap scored

1 garlic clove, finely chopped

2 teaspoons chopped rosemary

⅛ teaspoon freshly ground black pepper

1¼ teaspoons sea salt, divided

1 tablespoon white miso paste

¼ teaspoon smoked paprika

5 tablespoons unsalted butter, softened, divided

2 medium Yukon gold potatoes

1 teaspoon honey

¼ teaspoon ground coriander

½ lb. medium carrots, peeled

1 tablespoon finely chopped parsley

1. Preheat the oven to 425°F.

2. Rub lamb with garlic, rosemary, pepper, and ½ teaspoon salt.

3. In a small bowl, combine miso, paprika, 4 tablespoons butter, and ½ teaspoon salt, mix well, and set aside.

4. Peel the potatoes. Working with one potato at a time, slice a thin sliver off one long side to make a flat bottom. Trim ends off, then slice vertically every ⅟₁₆", cutting down to ¼" from the bottom. To make sure you do not cut all the way through the potato, line it with chopsticks on each side to stop your knife. Brush potatoes with miso butter, fanning slices open to get butter between each slice. Transfer to a rimmed baking sheet and roast for 15 minutes.

5. Remove the baking sheet from the oven and brush potatoes with more miso butter. Arrange lamb on baking sheet alongside potatoes and roast, brushing potatoes with miso butter halfway through, until an instant-read thermometer inserted into the thickest part of the lamb registers 125°F for medium-rare, and the potatoes are fork-tender, 20 to 25 minutes.

6. Transfer lamb to a cutting board and let rest for 10 minutes, and continue roasting the potatoes if needed.

7. Meanwhile, in a bowl, combine the honey, coriander, the remaining 1 tablespoon butter, and ¼ teaspoon salt, mix well, and then brush over carrots. Arrange carrots on a baking sheet and roast until lightly browned and fork-tender, 15 to 20 minutes.

8. Slice lamb between each rib. Brush potatoes with remaining miso butter, top carrots with parsley, and serve alongside lamb.

BRISKET WITH POMEGRANATE-WALNUT SAUCE & PISTACHIO GREMOLATA

Tart pomegranate, acting as both marinade and sauce, brings brightness and balance to this rich brisket. The gremolata adds a touch of herbal freshness.

YIELD: **8 Servings**

ACTIVE TIME: **30 Minutes**

TOTAL TIME: **30 Hours**

BRISKET AND MARINADE

1 (7 lb.) beef brisket with fat trimmed to ¼" thickness

2 teaspoons sea salt, plus more to taste

1 teaspoon freshly ground black pepper, plus more to taste

1 head of garlic, peeled

1 cup walnuts

2 tablespoons honey

3 cups pomegranate juice, divided

GREMOLATA

1½ cups mint leaves

½ cup shelled roasted and salted pistachios

2 garlic cloves

2 teaspoons lemon zest

¼ teaspoon sea salt

1/8 teaspoon freshly ground black pepper

2 tablespoons extra-virgin olive oil

1. Season brisket all over with salt and pepper. Transfer to a large 2-gallon resealable plastic bag or bowl.

2. Add garlic, walnuts, honey, and 1 cup pomegranate juice to a blender and puree until very smooth. Add remaining pomegranate juice and blend until smooth. Pour marinade over the brisket. Seal bag or cover bowl tightly with foil. Refrigerate for at least 24 hours, and up to 48 hours.

3. Transfer brisket and marinade to roasting pan, cover tightly with foil, and let sit at room temperature 1 hour.

4. Preheat the oven to 275°F.

5. Bake brisket, covered, until meat shreds easily with 2 forks, about 5 hours; if meat is still tough, continue cooking, covered, for 1 hour.

6. Transfer brisket to a cutting board and cover loosely with foil.

7. Transfer cooking liquid to a saucepan and spoon off fat from the surface. Cook over medium-high heat, skimming off fat and foam as it surfaces, until reduced by two-thirds, about 2 cups of sauce. Season with salt and pepper, if necessary.

8. Make the Gremolata by adding the mint, pistachios, garlic, lemon zest, salt, and pepper to a food processor and pulsing until coarsely chopped. Drizzle in oil, pulsing until just combined; do not overprocess.

9. To serve, slice the brisket against the grain and transfer to a platter. Spoon sauce over and top with Gremolata.

MSOKI DE PESAJ

The blend of braised lamb in a tomato-based stew makes this traditional Tunisian Passover dish a delicious dinner for cooler weather, as well.

YIELD: **6 Servings**

ACTIVE TIME: **45 Minutes**

TOTAL TIME: **3 Hours**

2½ lbs. lamb shoulder meat, chopped into 3" cubes

1 tablespoon kosher salt

½ teaspoon freshly ground black pepper

2 tablespoons avocado oil

2 large yellow onions, chopped

2 carrots, chopped

1 turnip, chopped

1 garlic clove, minced

1 cinnamon stick

2 teaspoons harissa

2 lbs. spinach leaves, finely chopped

2 leeks, finely chopped

1 zucchini, chopped

1 fennel, chopped

3 celery stalks, chopped

Half of 1 red kale lettuce heart, finely chopped

1½ cups fresh or frozen fava beans, defrosted

1 cup fresh or frozen green peas, defrosted

4 fresh or frozen artichoke hearts, defrosted and cut into wedges lengthwise

¼ bunch parsley, finely chopped

¼ bunch cilantro, finely chopped

¼ bunch mint leaves, finely chopped

2 teaspoons orange blossom water

1. Season the lamb with salt and pepper.

2. Add oil to a large pot over medium-high heat. When the oil is hot, sear the lamb until golden brown, about 3 to 5 minutes per side.

3. Add the onions, carrots, turnips, and garlic and sauté until soft and cooked, 15 to 20 minutes. Add the cinnamon stick and harissa and cook for about 5 more minutes.

4. Add the spinach, leeks, zucchini, fennel, celery, and red kale lettuce and continue cooking for another 15 minutes.

5. Add the fava beans, peas, artichoke hearts, parsley, cilantro, mint, and orange blossom water. Add enough water to reach three-quarters of the way up the vegetables. Simmer, uncovered, for about 2 hours, stirring occasionally, until the liquid has reduced to one-quarter the original amount.

6. Serve hot with rice.

POACHED FISH IN PEPPER SAUCE

This recipe is versatile and can be made with any type of white fish or salmon. Take the spice factor to a new level by adding harissa sauce or more chili powder, hot paprika, or red pepper flakes. A delightful main course for lunch over the Passover holiday.

YIELD: **6 Servings**

ACTIVE TIME: **15 Minutes**

TOTAL TIME: **30 Minutes**

2 lbs. white fish (such as tilapia, halibut, or flounder)

3 tablespoons avocado oil

2 garlic cloves, thinly sliced

2 medium onions, halved and thinly sliced

1 red pepper, cored, seeded, and thinly sliced

1 orange pepper, cored, seeded, and thinly sliced

1 yellow pepper cored, seeded, and thinly sliced

¼ teaspoon paprika

¾ teaspoon sea salt

Black pepper, to taste

¼-½ teaspoon your choice of chili powder, hot paprika, crushed red pepper flakes

1½ cups water

⅔ cup chopped cilantro leaves

1. Cut the fish into 2" x 5" pieces. Set aside.

2. Add oil to a large frying pan over medium-low heat. Add the garlic and onions and cook for 5 minutes. Add the peppers and cook for another 4 minutes.

3. Stir in the paprika, salt, black pepper, and chili powder or heat of choice. Add the water, increase the heat to medium-high, and bring to a boil.

4. Reduce the heat to low, place the fish slices on top of the garlic, onions, and peppers, cover, and cook for 5 minutes.

5. Use a fork to place some of the peppers and onions on top of the fish. Cover and cook for another 5 minutes. Taste the sauce and add more salt if necessary.

6. Sprinkle with the cilantro and serve.

STUFFED LAMB

This stuffed lamb recipe is ideal for a more decadent Passover spread. The complex sauce is rich and delicately sweet and spicy.

YIELD: **6 to 8 Servings**

ACTIVE TIME: **40 Minutes**

TOTAL TIME: **2 hours and 50 Minutes**

SAUCE

2 lbs. (8 small) roma tomatoes, halved lengthwise and quartered

½ cup tomato paste

3 tablespoons tamarind concentrate

1 tablespoon avocado oil

1 tablespoon sugar

4 garlic cloves, minced

2 small dried chile de árbol

1 large yellow onion, roughly chopped

1½ cups pitted kalamata olives

1 cup fresh cilantro leaves

Sea salt, to taste

STUFFING

2 tablespoons avocado oil

1 large yellow onion, finely chopped

3 garlic cloves, minced

1½ bs. ground lamb

1 cup long-grain white rice

5 small dried chile de árbol

1 small plum tomato, roughly chopped

1 Pinch freshly grated nutmeg

Sea salt, to taste

2 cups beef broth

1 cup water

BRAISED LAMB

1 (3½ lb.) lamb shoulder

2 tablespoons avocado or grapeseed oil

4 celery stalks, roughly chopped

2 large carrots, roughly chopped

1 large yellow onion, roughly chopped

3 cups beef broth

Sea salt, to taste

POTATOES

1 lb. small new potatoes, preferably multi-color

½ cup cilantro stems

Sauce

1. Combine the tomatoes, tomato paste, tamarind concentrate, oil, sugar, garlic, chiles, and onion in a medium saucepan and cook over low heat until the tomatoes break down and the sauce reduces, about 1 hour and 30 minutes.

2. Add the olives and cilantro, then cook until the olives soften, another 30 minutes.

3. Season with salt to taste and set aside.

Stuffing

1. Heat the oil in a heavy-bottomed pan over medium heat and sweat the onions and garlic until translucent, 4 to 5 minutes. Add the ground lamb, rice, chiles, tomato, and nutmeg, then stir, breaking up the ground lamb, until the lamb is browned, 3 to 4 minutes. Season with salt to taste.

2. Add the broth to the mixture and bring to a simmer. Cook until the liquid almost completely evaporates, 10 to 12 minutes. Add the water and return to a simmer. Cook again until the water almost completely evaporates, about 8 minutes. Reduce the heat to low and cover the pan. Cook until the rice is tender, about 5 minutes more. Fluff with a fork and check for seasoning.

Braised Lamb

1. Preheat the oven to 375°F. Butterfly the lamb shoulder so that it is one, large piece, even in thickness (you can ask the butcher to do this for you). Season both sides generously with salt.

2. Place 1 cup of stuffing in a row down the center of the lamb and roll into a log. Tie the lamb into a roast with twine. Reserve the remaining stuffing for serving.

3. Heat the oil in a 6-quart Dutch oven over medium-high heat. Sear the lamb, turning as needed, until browned on all sides, 15 to 18 minutes. Transfer the lamb to a plate.

4. Reduce the heat to medium and add the celery, carrots, and onion to the pan. Cook until the vegetables are slightly brown, 6 to 8 minutes. Add the broth and deglaze, scraping up any browned bits on the bottom of the pan with a wooden spoon.

5. Return the lamb to the pot and bring to a simmer. Cover the pot and transfer to the oven. Braise until the lamb is tender and reads 145°F on a thermometer, around 50 to 55 minutes. Transfer the lamb to a platter and cover with foil to rest.

Potatoes

1. Place the potatoes and cilantro stems in a medium saucepan. Strain the braising liquid, discarding the vegetables and transfer to pot with the potatoes. Bring to a boil and cook until the potatoes are tender when pierced with a knife, 20 minutes.

2. Layer the remaining stuffing on a large platter. Slice the lamb, discarding the twine and arrange over the stuffing. Scatter the potatoes around the lamb and spoon some of the braising liquid over top. Serve with the tomato-olive sauce on the side.

MINA DE ESPINACA

Matzo is truly the gift that keeps on giving. This pie—which, if you ask us, looks a lot like Jewish lasagna—uses softened matzo to create layers filled with a delicious cheese and spinach.

YIELD: **6 Servings**

ACTIVE TIME: **30 Minutes**

TOTAL TIME: **1 Hour and 30 Minutes**

2 russet potatoes

1 tablespoon plus
2¾ teaspoons sea salt,
divided

1¼ cups grated Parmesan
cheese, divided

1 (8 oz.) block cream cheese

2 eggs, lightly beaten

1 lb. baby spinach, regular
spinach or defrosted frozen
spinach, finely chopped

8 matzo sheets

1½ tablespoons plus
1 teaspoon avocado oil,
divided

1. Place the potatoes into a pot. Cover with room temperature water, add 1 tablespoon salt, and bring to a boil over high heat. Reduce the heat to medium-low and cook for 20 to 25 minutes, until the potatoes can be easily pierced with a knife. Drain the potatoes and cool for about 5 minutes until the potatoes are still warm but easier to handle. Peel the potatoes; discard the peels.

2. In a large bowl, mash the potatoes with a potato ricer or fork, until smooth with no chunks. Add 1½ teaspoons salt, ¾ cup Parmesan, cream cheese, and the beaten eggs to the potatoes. Mix well with a spatula until the mixture is smooth and uniform. Set aside.

3. In a large bowl, combine the spinach with ¼ cup Parmesan and 1 teaspoon salt. Mix until the salt and cheese are evenly distributed with the spinach. Set aside.

4. Preheat the oven to 350°F. Grease a 10" circular springform baking pan with 1 teaspoon oil.

5. Fill a container large enough to fit one matzo sheet with water halfway up to the rim and ¼ teaspoon salt. Soak the matzo, one sheets at a time, in the water for about 30 seconds, until each sheet is flexible yet still firm enough to hold its shape. Gently place each soaked matzo on a kitchen towel and remove any excess moisture. Set aside.

6. Line the bottom of the baking pan with two matzos, one on top of the other. Trim any edges as needed and use the trimmings to fill in any gaps. Evenly spread half of the spinach-parmesan mixture on top of the matzos. Add another double layer of moistened matzos on top of the spinach and gently press the matzos into the spinach layer to make space for the remaining layers. Spread the second half of the spinach mixture over the matzo layer. Place another double layer of matzo over the second spinach layer. Gently press the matzos into the spinach to make room for the remaining layer. Spread the potato mixture evenly over the matzo layer. Use the back of a spoon or an offset spatula to make swirls on the surface of the potatoes to brown evenly in the oven. Sprinkle the remaining ¼ cup Parmesan on top of the potato mixture and drizzle 1½ tablespoons oil on top.

7. Bake the assembled mina for 35 to 45 minutes, until the mina is deeply golden brown.

8. Allow the mina to cool for about 5 minutes. Run the tip of a sharp knife along the outside edges of the mina to separate it from the pan. Unmold and serve hot.

MAROR

On Passover, Jews eat horseradish to remember the bitterness of their forebears' lives as slaves in ancient Egypt. Regular horseradish is too mild to do justice to the experience, so making your own maror is a must. The great news is that it's so easy, you can eat it year-round instead of buying the bottled stuff. Just watch out for your eyes and don't come kvetching to us if you breathe in the fumes.

YIELD: **1 Cup**

ACTIVE TIME: **10 Minutes**

TOTAL TIME: **10 Minutes**

1 cup peeled and cubed horseradish root

¾ cup red or white wine vinegar (depending on your preference for color)

2 teaspoons sugar

¼ teaspoon salt

1. Combine all of the ingredients in a food processor or blender, and then process until the mixture is pureed. Cover the horseradish and refrigerate to store.

COCONUT MACAROONS

A Passover staple because they have no flour or leavening, macaroons were originally made with an almond base before the coconut version became an American tradition. You don't have to wait for the holidays to enjoy these now-classic treats.

YIELD: **10 Servings**

ACTIVE TIME: **10 Minutes**

TOTAL TIME: **45 Minutes**

Butter and flour for preparing baking sheet and foil

1 pinch almond flour, for dusting

1 large egg white

1 tablespoon sugar

¼ teaspoon vanilla

⅛ teaspoon almond extract

¾ cup sweetened flaked coconut

1. Put the oven rack in the middle position and preheat the oven to 300°F. Butter a baking sheet, then line with foil and lightly butter and flour foil, knocking off excess flour.

2. Stir together egg white, sugar, vanilla, almond extract, and a pinch of salt until combined, then stir in coconut. Divide coconut mixture into fourths, then drop in 4 mounds (about 2" apart) onto the baking sheet.

3. Bake until the tops are pale golden in spots, 15 to 20 minutes, then carefully lift foil with cookies from baking sheet and transfer to a rack to cool completely, about 15 minutes. Peel macaroons from foil.

CHEESECAKE, page 184

CHEESECAKE

Considered one of the earliest recipes that the Central European Jewish community assimilated, now the world associates cheesecake with New York City. And who can blame them? It's rumored that the original deli cheesecake came from Lindy's on Broadway before being picked up by Jewish-owned Kraft as a way to sell their cream cheese. The rest is dense-yet-pillowy history when it comes to this rich dessert only made more perfect by a simple fruit topping.

YIELD: **8 Servings**

ACTIVE TIME: **1 Hour**

TOTAL TIME: **10 Hours**

CRUST

1 tablespoon unsalted butter, softened

⅓ cup cake flour, sifted

¾ teaspoon baking powder

⅛ teaspoon sea salt

2 extra-large yolks, separated

⅓ cup granulated white sugar

CAKE

1¼ teaspoons pure vanilla extract, plus 1 tablespoon, divided

2 tablespoons unsalted butter, melted

¼ teaspoon cream of tartar

4 (8 oz.) packages of cream cheese

1⅔ cups granulated sugar, divided

¼ cup cornstarch

2 extra-large eggs

¾ cup heavy whipping cream

⅔ cups sour cream

1. Preheat the oven to 350°F.

2. Butter the bottom and side of a 9" springform pan.

3. Wrap the outside with aluminum foil, covering the bottom and extending it all the way up the side.

4. In a bowl, sift the flour, baking powder, and sea salt together.

5. In a bowl, using an electric mixer, beat the egg yolks on high for 2½ minutes.

6. With the mixer running, slowly add 2 tablespoons sugar and continue beating until thick, light-yellow ribbons form in the bowl, about 5 minutes more.

7. Mix in 1¼ teaspoons vanilla extract.

8. Sift the flour mixture over the batter and stir it in by hand, just until there are no remaining white flecks.

9. Blend in the melted butter.

10. In another bowl, beat the egg whites and cream of tartar together on high until frothy.

11. Gradually add the remaining sugar and continue beating until stiff peaks form.

12. Fold about one-third of the egg whites into the batter and then fold in the remaining egg whites.

13. Spread the batter over the bottom of the prepared pan and bake until just set and golden, about 10 minutes.

14. Remove pan from oven and set aside to cool.

15. In a bowl, using an electric mixer, beat 1 package of the softened cream cheese, ⅓ cup sugar, and the cornstarch together on low speed until creamy, about 3 minutes, scraping the bottom and sides of the bowl several times during the mixing process.

16. Blend in the remaining cream cheese, 1 package at a time, beating well and scraping down the bottom of the bowl several times after each block.

17. Increase the mixer speed to medium and beat in the remaining sugar, then add the vanilla and mix again. Increase mixer speed and continue to blend batter

18. Blend in the eggs, 1 egg at a time, beating well after each egg.

19. Beat in the heavy whipping cream until just completely blended.

20. Preheat the oven to 350°F.

21. Gently spoon the batter over the crust.

22. Place the cake pan in a large shallow pan. Make a water bath by adding enough hot water so it comes halfway up the side of the springform pan. Bake for about 1 hour and 15 minutes.

23. The cheesecake edges should look golden brown, and the center should be a lighter golden. If the center looks too soft, bake for an additional 8 minutes.

24. Remove the cheesecake from the water bath, let cool for 2 hours, and then cover with plastic wrap and refrigerate overnight.

25. Serve cold with a fresh fruit compote.

FLOURLESS CHOCOLATE CAKE

Even on Passover, when flour is forbidden, chocolate cake is not. This is a staple recipe to always have at the ready.

YIELD: **16 Servings**

ACTIVE TIME: **50 Minutes**

TOTAL TIME: **1 Hour and 25 Minutes**

4 large eggs, separated

10 tablespoons butter, cubed

1/2 cup sugar, divided

6 oz. semisweet chocolate, chopped

3 oz. unsweetened chocolate, chopped

2 teaspoons vanilla extract

1/4 cup finely ground pecans, toasted

Sliced strawberries and fresh mint, for garnish (optional)

1. Let egg whites stand at room temperature for 30 minutes. In a heavy saucepan, melt butter, ¼ cup sugar and chocolates over low heat, stirring constantly. Cool until the mixture is lukewarm.

2. In a large bowl, beat egg yolks until thick and lemon-colored, about 3 minutes. Beat in vanilla. Gradually beat in pecans and chocolate mixture.

3. In a small bowl and with clean beaters, beat egg whites on medium speed until soft peaks form. Gradually add remaining sugar, 1 tablespoon at a time, beating on high speed until stiff peaks form. Stir a small amount of whites into the chocolate mixture. Fold in remaining whites.

4. Pour into a greased 9" springform pan. Place on a baking sheet and bake at 350°F for 40 to 50 minutes or until a toothpick inserted in the center comes out with a few moist crumbs. Cool on a wire rack for 20 minutes.

5. Carefully run a knife around the edge of the pan to loosen; remove sides of pan and cool completely. Frost with Chocolate Ganache if desired. Garnish with strawberries and mint if desired.

HANUKKAH

IN LATE FALL AND EARLY WINTER, when the days have become their shortest and sunshine is scarce, along comes Hanukkah, the Festival of Lights. Winter celebrations in many cultures and religions commemorate the returning of light on or around winter solstice, but Hanukkah, like most Jewish holidays, is historical before being seasonal. The Hanukkah story begins with a second-century BCE fight between the Jewish people and their oppressors that led to the Maccabees' revolt, Jerusalem being recovered by the Jewish people, and the rededication of the Second Temple.

But you can't talk about Hanukkah without discussing oil. Because the holiday itself honors the miracle of the oil; when the Second Temple was back under Jewish control, it was discovered that much of what remained inside had been ruined or desecrated. This included ritual oil that was used to keep the Temple's menorah lit. There was only enough oil to light the menorah for one day, yet it burned for a miraculous eight days, enough time to have a new oil press made. Thus, an eight-night celebration that includes lighting the candles of a nine-branch menorah called a hanukkiah was born.

Now, let's talk food. The miracle of the oil is taken quite literally here, and foods deep-fried in oil are on the menu. No Hanukkah celebration would be complete without latkes, the crispy, fried potato pancakes that are a beloved staple of Ashkenazi cuisine. The debate on whether or not to eat with applesauce or sour cream can be, in some families, as hot as the oil they're fried in.

In Israel, a Hanukkah favorite is the sufganiyot, the original jelly doughnut. Sufganiyot is fried dough filled with jelly or custard and then sprinkled with powdered sugar. Although wildly popular amongst Israelis around the Festival of Lights, this treat originated in Europe around the 1500s and became known as the Berliner. For history buffs, yes, this is the famous jelly doughnut JFK accidentally referenced during his "Ich bin ein Berliner" speech—little did he know, his grammatical faux pas was linked to Hanukkah!

Sephardic tradition has its own version of the sufganiyot, the bimuelos or buñuelos. These decadent treats can be a dough fried up in a ball, or served flat and extra crispy. They can be served with sprinkled sugar, honey, cinnamon, or lightly perfumed with orange blossom water.

Other Hanukkah staples might include braided challah, brisket, couscous, or a variety of fried dishes (fritto misto, anyone?). And many an Ashkenazi celebration will also feature chocolate coins for children. The shiny gold and silver paper shimmers in such a way to tie into the theme of lights, of course. But the coins themselves harken back to Eastern European shtetls, where it was customary to tip workers around this time of the year with Hanukkah gelt.

A Hanukkah fact of note: in Western popular culture at least, Hanukkah seems to be the most well-known and celebrated Jewish holiday of the year. But for Jews, Hanukkah is a minor, yet beloved, festival. Non-Jewish familiarity with the eight-day celebration likely stems from it falling around the same time of the year as Christmas. But with the many lights, fried foods, and boisterous celebrating, it has little-to-nothing in common with Christmas. It's Jewish Independence Day!

LATKES

Often served on Hanukkah, latkes are essentially fried potato pancakes topped with anything from sour cream to applesauce. The tradition of the latke is focused on the oil rather than the potato. It symbolizes the miracle of Hanukkah when, thousands of years ago, one night's oil lasted for eight nights.

YIELD: **12 Servings**

ACTIVE TIME: **20 Minutes**

TOTAL TIME: **45 Minutes**

1 lb. russet potatoes, grated

1 large onion, grated

3 large eggs

½ cup all-purpose flour

2 teaspoons sea salt

1 teaspoon baking powder

½ teaspoon freshly ground black pepper

Avocado oil, for frying

1. Combine the potatoes and onion is a large cheesecloth-lined bowl and squeeze out as much liquid as possible.

2. Transfer the mixture to a large dry bowl, add the eggs, flour, salt, baking powder, and pepper, and mix until the flour is absorbed.

3. In a medium heavy-bottomed pan over medium-high heat, pour in about ¼" of oil.

4. Once the oil is hot, drop tablespoons of batter into the hot pan, being sure not to overcrowd the pan, and use a spatula to flatten and shape the drops into pancakes.

5. When the edges of the latkes are brown and crispy, about 5 minutes, flip, and cook until the second side is deeply browned, about another 5 minutes.

6. Transfer the latkes to a paper towel-lined plate to drain and sprinkle with salt while still warm.

7. Repeat with the remaining batter.

8. Serve with sour cream or applesauce.

POT ROAST

Slow cooked until tender and delicious, this is comfort food at its finest, no matter the occasion.

YIELD: **6 Servings**

ACTIVE TIME: **30 Minutes**

TOTAL TIME: **3 Hours and 30 Minutes**

---

1 (3-5 lb.) beef roast chuck or bottom round

2 teaspoons sea salt

1 teaspoon black pepper

3 garlic cloves, peeled and smashed

1 cup red wine

2 cups Beef Stock (see page 246)

1 tablespoon Worcestershire sauce

1 onion, halved

1 lb. carrots, sliced on bias into spears

½ head of celery, cut into 3" spears

1 lb. Yukon gold potatoes, halved

2 tablespoons tomato paste

1 teaspoon sweet paprika

¼ cup plus 3 tablespoons avocado oil

1 bay leaf

1 sprig fresh rosemary

2 cloves, whole studded into onion

1 leek, halved

1. Preheat the oven to 350°F and set a Dutch oven over high heat.

2. Season both sides of meat with salt and pepper. Add oil to the pot and sear meat on all sides until browned, about 3 to 4 minutes per side.

3. Remove roast from pan and set aside. Add garlic to pot and cook for 1 minute, and then deglaze the pot with red wine and stock. Add meat back to the pot.

4. Pour Worcestershire sauce over the meat and place the onion, carrots, celery, potatoes, and the rest of the ingredients on top of and around the meat.

5. Place a lid on the pan and transfer it to the oven. Cook 3 hours, or until meat reaches an internal temperature of 202°F and is fork-tender and easy to slice.

6. Season vegetables with additional salt and pepper to taste and serve hot.

KEFTES DE ESPINACA

Small fried patties or croquettes, known as keftes, are popular in the Sephardic Jewish community. These are a delicious vegetarian take on the usually meaty kefte concept. Because keftes are pan fried in oil, they are often served for Hanukkah.

YIELD: **12 Servings**

ACTIVE TIME: **15 Minutes**

TOTAL TIME: **30 Minutes**

½ cup plus 1 tablespoon avocado oil

1 onion, minced

½ teaspoon crushed garlic

10 oz. fresh spinach leaves

1 large egg

1 cup mashed russet potatoes

½ cup plain bread crumbs or matzo meal

1 teaspoon sea salt

¼ teaspoon black pepper

1 pinch cayenne (optional)

1. Add 1 tablespoon oil to a large skillet over medium heat. Sauté minced onion for 5 minutes until translucent. Add crushed garlic, sauté for 2 minutes longer.

2. Add half of the fresh spinach and allow the spinach to wilt and shrink slightly, then add remaining half and cover again, until all of the spinach has wilted.

3. Remove from heat and transfer the cooked mixture to a mesh strainer. With a spatula, gently press mixture in the strainer to remove excess moisture. Transfer mixture to a cutting board and roughly chop.

4. Place chopped mixture into a mixing bowl. Add remaining ingredients and mix well.

5. With an ice cream scoop or ¼ cup measuring cup, scoop the mixture into your hand and form smooth flat patties. Place them onto a sheet tray as you go.

6. Add remaining oil to the skillet over medium heat and bring to about 365°F. Place patties into the hot oil in small batches. Fry until brown, about 4 minutes on each side. Place on a paper towel or rack to drain.

7. Serve immediately.

BOUREKAS, page 200

BOUREKAS

The thin and flaky pastry is usually made from phyllo or yufka dough. The potato and cheese filling is simple enough to make, which is good news considering that these savory bites will be requested again and again.

YIELD: **12 Servings**

ACTIVE TIME: **1 Hour**

TOTAL TIME: **1 Hour and 50 Minutes**

---

3 medium Yukon gold potatoes, peeled and cut into 1" pieces

2 tablespoons extra-virgin olive oil

1 small onion, chopped

1 garlic clove, minced

⅛ teaspoon ground nutmeg

1 cup ricotta cheese

1 cup grated kashkaval cheese

Sea salt, to taste

Freshly ground black pepper, to taste

2 large eggs

1 (14-16 oz.) package puff pastry (sheets or pre-cut squares)

Toasted sesame seeds, for sprinkling

1. Place the potatoes in a stockpot with enough cold water to cover by 1". Bring to a boil over medium-high heat and cook uncovered until the potatoes are tender and easily pierced with a fork, about 25 minutes.

2. Drain potatoes, place in a bowl, and mash with a potato masher. Set aside to cool.

3. Add oil to a skillet set over medium-high heat and sauté onion and garlic until soft and translucent, about 7 minutes. Remove from heat and set aside.

4. In a bowl, combine the nutmeg and cheeses and mix well.

5. Add the onion mixture and the cheese mixture to the potatoes, mix well, and season to taste with salt and pepper.

6. In a bowl, beat one of the eggs.

7. While stirring the cool potato mixture, slowly add the beaten egg. Mix well until the egg is totally integrated into the mashed potatoes.

8. Preheat the oven to 375°F.

9. Line a large baking sheet with parchment paper. Fill a bowl with water.

10. Cut puff pastry sheets into 5" squares.

11. Place a heaping tablespoon of filling in the center of each square.

12. Dip your fingers in the water and dampen the edges of the squares, then fold in half vertically to form a triangle pastry. Pinch the edges together to seal the filling inside.

13. Beat the second egg and brush it over the tops of the bourekas. Sprinkle sesame seeds on top.

14. Bake for 30 minutes, or until the bourekas are puffed and golden.

LATKES WITH SHORT RIBS

Latkes are the perfect side dish year-round, not only for Hanukkah celebrations. Try this pairing and discover that the sauce and spice from the short ribs are ideally matched with crispy, golden potato pancakes.

YIELD: **6 Servings**

ACTIVE TIME: **1 Hour**

TOTAL TIME: **3 Hours**

2 lbs. bone-in short ribs, cut across the bone into 2½" pieces

1½ tablespoons sea salt

½ teaspoon ground black pepper

2 tablespoons avocado oil

5 allspice berries

1 yellow onion, finely chopped

2 garlic cloves, finely chopped

LATKES

1 yellow onion

4 large russet potatoes

1 tablespoon all-purpose flour

½ cup thinly sliced scallion

1 whole egg

1 egg yolk

1½ tablespoons sea salt

½ teaspoon freshly ground black pepper

Avocado oil, for frying

3-5 sprigs fresh dill or parsley

1. Season the short ribs with salt and pepper.

2. Add oil to a large pot over medium-high heat. Once the oil is hot, gently add the short ribs and sear on all sides until golden brown, about 5 minutes per side.

3. Transfer the meat to a plate and reduce the heat to medium. Add the onions and garlic and sauté until soft, about 15 minutes.

4. Return the meat to the pot, along with the allspice and add enough water to cover the beef about three-quarters of the way up. Bring the mixture to a boil, then reduce the heat and simmer, covered, for about 3 hours, or until the meat is tender and the liquid has reduced to a stew-like consistency.

5. For the latkes, grate the onion and potatoes and wrap them in a tea towel and squeeze out as much liquid as possible into a bowl. After about 5 minutes the potato starch in the liquid will settle at the bottom of the bowl. Gently drain out the water and then scrape off the potato starch from the bowl.

6. In a separate bowl, combine the potato starch, onions, potatoes, flour, eggs, salt, and pepper and mix well.

7. Preheat the oven to 400°F.

8. Add about 1" of oil to a large skillet over medium-high heat. Once the oil is sizzling, take 1½ tablespoons of the potato mixture into your palm and shape into a flat disk that is about 3" wide. Gently place the latke into the oil. Repeat the process, adding 4 or 5 more latkes to the pan, being sure to not overcrowd the pan. Fry the latkes on both sides until golden brown, about 5 minutes per side. Transfer to a paper towel-lined plate and continue frying the latkes in batches.

9. Once the stew is ready, arrange the latkes in one layer in a baking pan. Once the short ribs are cool enough to handle, shred the beef and discard the bones. Gently place a dollop of meat over each latke. Pour the stew liquids over the latkes. Place the baking pan in the oven and reduce the heat to 350°F. Bake for 15 minutes, or until the latkes have absorbed some of the stew and the flavors of the beef.

10. Serve hot with a few sprigs of fresh dill or parsley.

SHORT RIBS

2 tablespoons avocado oil

3 lbs. English-cut beef short ribs (or 2 lbs. stew beef)

1 large onion, chopped

½ cup dry red wine

8 cups Beef Stock (see page 246)

BORSCHT

4 large beets, peeled and diced

1 large russet potato, peeled and cut into ½" cubes

2 celery ribs, diced

1 small rutabaga, peeled and diced

1 lb. carrots, diced

3 teaspoons olive oil

½ tablespoon whole black peppercorns

½ tablespoon whole coriander seeds

2 Sprigs fresh dill

2 sprigs fresh oregano

2 sprigs fresh Italian flat leaf parsley

2 tablespoons avocado oil

1 leek, diced

1 large onion, diced

2 cups thinly sliced cabbage

7 oz. can chopped tomatoes and their juices

½ cup dry red wine

2 tablespoons red wine vinegar

Sea salt, to taste

Freshly ground pepper, to taste

Dill, for serving

Grated horseradish, for serving

BEEF, BEET & CABBAGE BORSCHT

Although variants of this pleasantly sour-tasting soup exist without beets, most have come to know this Eastern European staple by the deep-red root vegetable that imparts such a distinctive color.

1. Prepare the short ribs by heating oil in a large, thick-bottomed pot over medium high heat. Add the short ribs or stew beef and brown lightly on one side, then turn over.

2. Add the onions and cook for about 5 minutes. Add the wine and stock and bring to a boil. Cover and simmer, stirring occasionally, until the meat is very tender, about 2 hours. Skim off excess fat from the liquid in the pot. Remove the meat to a baking sheet, let cool, and dice. Strain the broth and reserve; discard the bones and other solids.

3. Preheat the oven to 400°F.

4. Toss the beets, potatoes, celery, rutabaga, and carrots with olive oil and spread them out in a single layer on a foil-lined roasting pan. Roast for 15 minutes.

5. Wrap the peppercorns, coriander seeds, dill, oregano, and parsley sprigs in cheesecloth and tie into a bundle.

6. In a large pot, heat the avocado oil. Add the beets, rutabaga, leek, onion, carrots, celery, cabbage and the herb-spice bundle. Cook, stirring occasionally, until the cabbage is wilted, about 15 minutes. Add the tomatoes and wine and simmer for about 5 minutes.

7. Stir in the strained beef broth and simmer for about 30 minutes. Stir in the vinegar and the meat and simmer for 15 minutes. Season with salt and pepper.

8. Serve the borscht with chopped dill and horseradish.

TIP: The beauty of this soup is the shapes of the beets, carrots and other root vegetables that shine in the bowl. This is a great way to practice knife skills, try your best to make square dice and other varieties of shapes with the root vegetables. As an alternative cooking methodology; try roasting beets whole on a bed of kosher salt, then peel and cut after they've cooled. This cooking method will enhance the flavors of beet and draw out moisture.

BEEF BRISKET

Made with one of the toughest cuts of a butchered cow—and back in the shtetls of Eastern Europe the most inexpensive—this recipe yields a perfect brisket every single time, and is testament to the power of simple cooking.

YIELD: **15 Servings**

ACTIVE TIME: **45 Minutes**

TOTAL TIME: **5 Hours**

5 tablespoons avocado oil

1 whole beef brisket (5-7 lbs.), trimmed of excess fat

2 teaspoons sea salt

1 teaspoon freshly ground black pepper

2 large onions, roughly chopped

2 large garlic cloves, minced

2 tablespoons dark brown sugar

2 tablespoons Worcestershire sauce

1 tablespoon dry mustard

1 tablespoon white vinegar

1 teaspoon chili powder

½ teaspoon paprika

1 (14 oz.) bottle of ketchup

1¼ cups water

2 large bay leaves

1. Preheat the oven to 350°F.

2. Add oil to a 10 or 12" sauté pan over high heat. Place the trimmed brisket in the hot oil, fat-side down, and cook until browned, 5 to 7 minutes. Season the brisket with ½ teaspoon salt and ¼ teaspoon pepper. Turn over the brisket and brown the other side. Season this side with the same amount of salt and pepper. If the brisket is too large to fit the pan, cut off the tip and brown it separately.

3. Meanwhile, in a large mixing bowl, combine the onions, garlic, brown sugar, Worcestershire, mustard, vinegar, chili powder, paprika, remaining salt and pepper, ketchup, and 1¼ cups water. Use some of the water to rinse out the ketchup bottle. Stir until well blended.

4. Transfer the browned and seasoned brisket to a roasting pan or Dutch oven just big enough to hold the meat with about an inch of space around it. Place the bay leaves on top of the meat and pour the ketchup mixture over it.

5. Cover the roasting pan (using aluminum foil if the pan doesn't have a lid) and roast for 2 hours.

6. Remove from the oven and uncover. When the brisket is cool enough to handle, transfer it to a cutting board. Slice the brisket on an angle across the grain. The slices should be less than ¼" thick. As you slice the meat, transfer the slices back to the cooking liquid. When all of the meat is sliced, pour any juice on the cutting board back into the roasting pan, re-cover it, and return it to the oven for 1½ to 2 hours, or until the meat is tender enough to cut with a fork. Remove from the oven and let cool slightly before serving.

7. To store, lift the meat out of the gravy and store separately. To reheat, layer the meat with some of the gravy, cover, and bake in a 325°F oven for 30 to 45 minutes, or until warm.

TSYPLYONOK TABAKA

This Russian dish of pressed and pan-fried Cornish hens is wonderful for Hanukkah. The walnut-garlic sauce is both pungent and lightly sweet.

YIELD: **2 Servings**

ACTIVE TIME: **1 Hour**

TOTAL TIME: **10 Hours**

WET RUB

1 cup avocado oil

6 garlic cloves, heavily smashed

1 tablespoon turmeric

1 tablespoon smoked paprika

1 tablespoon freshly ground pepper

1 tablespoon garlic powder

Juice and peel of one lemon (peel to be in strips, made with a vegetable peeler)

Juice and peel of one orange (peel to be in strips, made with a vegetable peeler)

1 medium white onion, sliced into thin rings

CHICKEN

2 (1½-2 lb.) Cornish hens, poussins, or small chickens

6 garlic cloves, peeled and smashed

1 handful each of roughly chopped dill, cilantro, tarragon, flat-leaf parsley, mixed

6 tablespoons clarified butter, divided

2 tablespoons avocado oil, divided

Juice from ½ a lemon

Walnut-Garlic Sauce, for serving

1. In a bowl, combine all of the ingredients for the wet rub and mix well.

2. Rinse and pat dry the chickens. Spatchcock each chicken: cut out the backbone of each bird using poultry shears; open like a book, remove the breast bones, and flatten with the palm of your hand.

3. Cover them in plastic wrap and use the flat side of a meat mallet to pound the chickens and flatten them further, especially in bony areas. Put the chickens in individual gallon resealable plastic bags.

4. Pour half of the spice paste into each bag and rub chickens all over and under the skin where it pulls away easily.

5. Separate the sliced onions across the 2 bags, and spread around all sides of the chickens.

6. Push out the air and seal. Refrigerate for 6 to 8 hours, preferably overnight.

7. Remove the chickens from the refrigerator and wipe off excess juices, discard any excess rub, garlic, and onions. Blot the chickens with paper towels to dry them as well as you can. Set over clean paper towels and let sit for 30 minutes at room temperature before cooking.

8. Preheat the oven to 200°F to keep cooked chicken warm while cooking remaining chicken, if necessary. Have a lined sheet pan with a rack ready to transfer the chicken to the oven.

9. Prepare a large cast-iron pan that will fit a flattened bird, allowing the complete surface area of the chicken to be in direct contact with the pan. You will also need something to weigh down the chicken evenly. A smaller sized cast iron pan that fits inside the larger one, filled with a heavy mortar and pestle, or large cans of tomatoes works well. You can also use a foil wrapped brick or two, or a round Dutch oven weighted with cans or water-filled jars.

10. Cut a piece of parchment paper that will fit completely over the chicken in the large pan you'll be cooking the bird in and set aside.

11. Heat 2 tablespoons clarified butter in the large cast-iron pan over medium-high heat. Rub the chicken all over with oil, salt, and pepper.

12. Add to the hot pan, skin-side up. Cover with parchment paper and weigh down. Do not touch it or move it around. After 12 to 15 minutes, remove the weights and parchment and flip the chicken over, skin-side down. Replace parchment paper and weights and cook for 12 to 15 minutes more. Do not touch it or move it around so as not to tear or disturb the skin until it's crispy and pulls away from the pan by itself. It is done when a thermometer inserted into the thickest part of the breast reads 165°F, or juices run clear when pierced with the tip of a knife.

13. Remove chicken from pan, place skin side up and transfer to lined sheet pan. Place in a warm oven while making the second one the same way.

14. While both chickens are warming, melt the remaining 2 tablespoons clarified butter in a small saucepan with smashed garlic cloves and a squeeze of lemon juice. Warm through until fragrant. Remove chickens from the oven and pour any juices from the chickens into the butter mixture.

15. Arrange chickens on a serving platter or on a clean sheet tray, drizzle with warmed butter and garlic mixture, and generously top with chopped mixed herbs.

16. Serve with pickled vegetables, fermented cabbage slaw, and Walnut Garlic Sauce.

BLINTZES WITH BERRY COMPOTE

Everything yummy rolled up in a flat pancake. The Jewish version of blintzes can be filled with anything from chocolate to mushrooms, meat, rice, or mashed potatoes and cheese. Although they're not part of any specific religious event, blintzes stuffed with a cheese filling and fried in oil are served on holidays such as Hanukkah as a symbolic and historic gesture.

YIELD: **8**

ACTIVE TIME: **1 Hour**

TOTAL TIME: **1 Hour and 35 Minutes**

BLINTZES

4 large eggs

½ cup water

½ cup milk

½ teaspoon sea salt

1 cup all-purpose flour

1 cup unsalted butter

FILLING

1 lb. farmers cheese, at room temperature

1 tablespoon unsalted butter, melted

1 large egg yolk, at room temperature

2 teaspoons vanilla extract

¼ cup sugar

BERRY COMPOTE

¼ cup black berries

¼ cup blueberries

¼ cup strawberries

1 tablespoon water

1 tablespoon sugar

Sour cream (optional)

1. In a bowl, beat together eggs, water, milk, salt, and flour until well-mixed. Let the mixture rest at room temperature for at least 30 minutes.

2. Heat a sauté pan and add a pat of butter.

3. Mix the batter again until smooth. Pour about ¼ cup batter into the pan and swirl it around. Make sure not to let it brown. Flip and cook the other side for a few seconds before turning it out of the pan and setting aside.

4. Repeat with remaining batter, placing pats of butter in the pan between each blintz.

5. After all of the blintzes have been made, place one on a work surface and spread 1½ tablespoons of filling in a line close to the edge nearest to you.

6. Fold blintz like an envelope, then roll up, and continue with remaining blintzes and filling.

7. Add butter to a skillet and fry the filled blintzes until golden brown.

8. Serve topped with the compote and sour cream, if desired.

Filling

1. In a bowl, combine cheese, butter, egg yolk, vanilla, and sugar and mix until the batter achieves a smooth texture.

Berry Compote

1. Place all of the ingredients in a small saucepan over medium heat. Once the mixture begins to bubble, reduce heat slightly and use a wooden spoon to muddle and mash the fruit. Continue cooking over medium-low heat for 12 minutes, occasionally mashing fruit to combine. Remove from heat and let cool.

SUFGANIYOT

Potatoes aren't the only thing Jewish people deep-fry on Hanukkah. In Israel, sufganiyot—perhaps the most delicious jelly doughnuts you'll ever know—are an even more popular way of celebrating than latkes.

YIELD: 21 Servings

ACTIVE TIME: 45 Minutes

TOTAL TIME: 3 Hours

3½ cups all-purpose flour

½ teaspoon sea salt

¼ cup sugar

1 tablespoon dry instant yeast

1 egg

3½ tablespoons unsalted butter, cubed

1¼ cups lukewarm milk

1 quart avocado oil

½ cup strawberry or raspberry jam, Nutella, or ready-made vanilla pudding

¼ cup powdered sugar

1. Sift the flour into a large mixing bowl. Add the salt and sugar and mix well. Add the yeast and mix.

2. Using a mixer fitted with a hook attachment, mix the flour mixture on low speed and add the egg and butter. Gradually add the warm milk and continue mixing for 8 to 10 minutes, until the dough is soft.

3. Shape the dough into a ball and place it in a clean, lightly oiled bowl. Cover with a clean kitchen towel or plastic wrap and let rise until doubled in size, about 2 hours.

4. Once the dough has risen, place dough on a lightly floured work surface and roll out the dough to a thickness of ¾". Using a 2" cookie cutter, cut circles out of the dough, as close to one another as possible.

5. Place the dough circles on a baking tray lined with parchment paper and cover with a clean kitchen towel. Allow to rise again for 20 minutes.

6. In the meantime, heat the oil in a Dutch oven until it reaches 325°F.

7. Gently add 4 dough circles into the oil and fry for 2 to 3 minutes on each side, until golden brown, but not too brown. Remove with a slotted spoon and place on a paper towel-lined plate. Repeat with remaining dough. Allow to cool slightly before filling.

8. Fill a piping bag with your desired filling. Using a sharp knife, make a small slit on the top of the sufganiyot. Place the piping bag inside the slit and fill until you can see the filling on top.

9. Sprinkle with powdered sugar before serving.

BIALY, page 216

BREAD

Bread in its many forms is considered a blessing to any table. From bialy to laffa, here are the many bread recipes to break and eat with family and friends, including some wonderful sweet options

BALSAMIC APPLE DATE CHALLAH

This beloved loaf of bread is made fashionable in this recipe that is intensified with a combination of sweet-and-sour balsamic-glazed apples and dates.

YIELD: **2 loaves**
ACTIVE TIME: **35 Minutes**
TOTAL TIME: **6 Hours**

DOUGH

1½ tablespoons yeast

½ cup sugar, plus 1 teaspoon, divided

1¼ cups lukewarm water

4½-5 cups bread flour

½ tablespoon salt

3 tablespoons honey

2 teaspoons vanilla

1 teaspoon cinnamon

¼ teaspoon nutmeg

¼ cup vegetable oil

2 whole eggs

FILLING

3 gala apples, peeled, cored, and diced

1 cup pitted and chopped dates

½ teaspoon salt

1 cinnamon stick

¼ cup water

¼ cup red wine

1 tablespoon sugar

2 tablespoons balsamic vinegar

TOPPING

1 egg, beaten

1 teaspoon honey

Coarse Sea salt, to taste (optional)

Cinnamon sugar, to taste (optional)

1. In a small bowl, combine the yeast, 1 teaspoon sugar, and lukewarm water. Stir and allow to stand until it becomes foamy on top, about 10 minutes.

2. In a large bowl or stand mixer fitted with whisk attachment, mix together 1½ cups flour, salt, remaining sugar, honey, vanilla, cinnamon, and nutmeg. Add the foamy water and yeast mixture to the flour mixture along with oil and mix thoroughly.

3. Add another cup of flour and the eggs and whisk until smooth.

4. Switch to the dough hook attachment if you are using a stand mixer. Add another 1½ cups flour and then remove from the bowl and place on a floured surface. Knead remaining flour into dough, continuing to knead for around 10 minutes.

5. Place dough in a greased bowl, cover with a damp towel, and allow to rise for 3 to 4 hours.

6. To make the filling, combine the apples, dates, salt, cinnamon stick, water, red wine, and sugar in a medium saucepan and bring to a boil. Lower heat to medium and simmer until the mixture is reduced, about 10 minutes. Add the vinegar and simmer for another 3 minutes.

7. Remove from heat and allow to cool for 5 minutes. Remove cinnamon sticks and place the filling in a food processor fitted with the blade attachment and pulse until smooth.

8. After the challah is done rising, cut the dough in half. To be as precise as possible, use a scale to measure the weight.

9. Using a rolling pin, roll out the first ball into a rectangle. Spread around half, perhaps slightly less, of the filling in an even layer, leaving ½" all around without filling. Working quickly, start rolling up the dough toward you. Try and keep the roll relatively tight as you go. Pinch the end when you finish.

10. Create a pinwheel shaped-challah by snaking the dough around and around in a circle around itself. When finished, tuck the end under the challah neatly and pinch lightly. This doesn't have to be perfect—remember, as long as it tastes good, almost no one (maybe except that judgmental great aunt) will care what it looks like. Place the loaf on a baking sheet to proof for the second rise before baking.

11. Repeat with the other half of the dough.

12. Preheat the oven to 350°F.

13. Allow challahs to rise another 45 minutes, or until you can see that both loaves have grown. Beat 1 egg with 1 teaspoon honey. Brush liberally over each challah. Top challah with coarse sea salt and cinnamon sugar, if desired.

14. Bake for 25 to 30 minutes, or until the middle looks like it has just set, and the color is golden.

BIALY

When it comes to the difference between bagels and bialys, why choose sides? All we know is that the little indentation in the top means more room for extra garlic, onions, or seeds, which we are clearly all for.

YIELD: **12 Bialys**
ACTIVE TIME: **1 Hour**
TOTAL TIME: **10 Hours**

DOUGH

7 cups unbleached bread flour

2¾ teaspoons salt

1¼ teaspoons instant yeast

½ teaspoon onion powder

2¼ cups water

FILLING

1 medium onion, peeled and quartered

1 teaspoon poppy seeds

⅛ teaspoon salt

3–4 grinds coarsely ground black pepper

1 tablespoon olive oil

Cornmeal, for pans

Dough

1. Combine the flour, salt, yeast, and onion powder in the bowl of a stand mixer and mix well by hand. Add the water and mix, using the dough hook attachment, until just combined, 1 or 2 minutes at low speed. Stop the mixer, cover the bowl, and let rest for 20 minutes.

2. Uncover the bowl and continue kneading at medium speed for 8 minutes, or until the dough is smooth and elastic.

3. Cover and refrigerate the dough overnight for a slow, cool rise to develop the dough's flavor.

4. The next day, divide the dough into 12 pieces (they'll weigh just under 4 ounces each) and round each into a ball. Place on a lightly oiled baking sheet, cover with greased plastic, and let rise at room temperature for 1 hour, or until puffy.

5. Preheat the oven to 475°F.

6. Pulse the onion in a food processor until very finely chopped, but not liquid. Add in the poppy seeds, salt, and pepper.

7. Heat the oil in a saucepan and cook the onion mixture for a few minutes over medium-low heat until the liquid cooks off and the onion is very slightly caramelized. Remove from heat and let cool.

8. Lightly sprinkle 2 baking sheets with cornmeal. Take each dough ball and stretch it into a bagel shape about 6" to 7" in diameter, without puncturing the center, and being sure to leave a wide, flat indentation where the hole would be. Place a few inches apart on the prepared baking sheets, 6 per pan. Place a scant teaspoon of the onion filling in the indentation and spread it out with your fingers. Don't overfill; a little goes a long way.

9. Bake for 8 to 10 minutes, until light golden brown. Remove the bialys from the oven and serve warm; or cool on a rack and save for toasting later.

   TIP: Resist the temptation to be generous with the onions; the moisture in them can keep the center of the bialy from cooking at the same speed as the edges, causing the center to puff up like a topknot.

CAST-IRON CHALLAH BREAD

Baked in cast-iron skillets, these loaves are dense, soft, and subtly sweet.

YIELD: **2 Loaves**

ACTIVE TIME: **30 Minutes**

TOTAL TIME: **3 Hours and 40 Minutes**

3 tablespoons active dry yeast

¾ cup sugar,
plus 1½ tablespoons

10 cups all-purpose flour,
plus more for dusting

¾ cup vegetable oil

1 tablespoon salt

2 eggs (1 whole, 1 separated)

Nonstick cooking spray

1. In a small bowl, dissolve yeast and 1½ tablespoons sugar in 2 cups warm water (110°F). Cover and set aside for 10 minutes or until bubbles form.

2. In the bowl of a stand mixer fitted with a dough hook, combine flour, remaining sugar, oil, salt, 1 whole egg, and 1 egg white. Mix at a very low speed for 5 minutes.

3. With the mixer running, slowly add the warm water and yeast mixture and continue to knead for 10 minutes.

4. The dough should feel soft and not too sticky. Transfer dough to an oiled bowl, cover with a towel, and allow to rest in a warm place for 1 hour, or until it has doubled in size. Punch down the dough, cover it, and let it rise again in a warm place for 30 minutes.

5. Coat two 8" cast-iron skillets with nonstick cooking spray.

6. Turn the dough out onto a lightly floured surface and divide into 8 equal balls. Roll each ball into a strand about 12" long. Weave 2 horizontal and 2 vertical strands to form a hashtag. Braid strands, moving right to left, always taking the strand underneath and crossing it over the next strand until a circle has formed. Repeat to form a second challah.

7. Tuck remaining ends under, and place each challah in one of the prepared cast-iron pans.

8. In a small bowl, beat together the remaining egg yolk and 1 teaspoon water; brush the top of each challah with egg wash.

9. Set pans in a warm place; allow dough to rise, uncovered, for 1 hour or until doubled in size.

10. Preheat the oven to 350°F.

11. Bake for 35 to 40 minutes, until golden brown. Let cool before serving.

CHALLAH FRENCH TOAST

Do people make French toast from anything else? Once you taste how day-old challah makes this classic breakfast treat something magical, you'll never use any other bread for this quick and easy recipe.

YIELD: **6 Servings**

ACTIVE TIME: **10 Minutes**

TOTAL TIME: **30 Minutes**

6 large eggs

2 cups whole milk

¼ cup sugar

1 vanilla bean, seeds scraped

1 pinch sea salt

1 loaf of Challah (see page 17), dried out or day-old, cut into ¾" slices

2 tablespoons unsalted butter, plus more as needed

Maple syrup, for serving

1. In a large bowl, combine the eggs, milk, sugar, vanilla bean seeds, and salt and whisk well.

2. Place the challah slices in a shallow baking dish and pour the egg mixture over the bread. Flip the bread over to absorb the egg mixture into both sides and let soak for 5 minutes. Refrigerate for 20 minutes before cooking; this will create a crispy texture and a light custard creamy texture on the inside.

3. Add 2 tablespoons butter to a cast-iron skillet over medium-high heat. When the butter is sizzling, add the soaked challah and lower the heat slightly. Cook 2 to 3 minutes on each side until golden brown. Repeat with the remaining bread adding more butter as needed. You can keep the finished slices warm on a sheet tray in the oven while cooking the remaining batches.

4. Serve hot with maple syrup.

CHOCOLATE BABKA, page 222

CHOCOLATE BABKA

This sweet cake is made from a dough that is doubled and twisted, and rises up to fluffy perfection thanks to yeast. Babka is filled with cinnamon and/or chocolate, which makes a marble pattern when sliced. It originates from Eastern Europe and was made known to the world thanks to that one *Seinfeld* episode.

YIELD: **4 Servings**

ACTIVE TIME: **1 Hour**

TOTAL TIME: **24 Hours**

DOUGH

½ oz. dried yeast

1 cup full-fat milk

½ cup sugar

2 eggs

4 cups all-purpose white flour (13.2% protein)

½ cup unsalted butter, cubed and softened

CHOCOLATE FILLING

2 cups roughly chopped 70% cocoa chocolate

¾ cup unsalted butter

½ cup sugar

2 tablespoons cocoa powder

½ cup chopped pistachios (reserved for sprinkling)

SUGAR SYRUP GLAZE

1¼ cups sugar

¼ cup water

1. Combine the yeast, milk, sugar, and eggs in the bowl of a stand mixer fitted with the dough hook and allow yeast to bloom. On a very low speed mix in flour, and when fully incorporated add the butter. Dough will be very sticky and elastic and will not want to form a ball. Mix until all the butter is dissolved into dough and smooth, about 15 minutes. Cover and refrigerate the dough overnight.

2. The next day, turn the dough out onto a clean work surface and fold it in over itself for 20 minutes, until the dough forms a ball. Use a bench scraper to assist in the folding process. The dough will be very sticky and you should avoid putting any extra flour on at this point. You want the dough to form a ball by creating gluten through the slap folding process. Slap the dough on the work surface and stretch it until elongated and fold it in on itself. Eventually, enough gluten will be created and the dough will become less sticky and actually form a smooth ball. Use a bench scraper to help form the ball.

3. Using a little oil on your hands turn the dough into a bowl and refrigerate it for 4 hours.

4. To make the filling, add all of the ingredients, setting aside ¼ cup chopped chocolate, to a small saucepan over medium heat and cook until well combined. Allow the chocolate to cool to room temperature before using or the dough will become sticky and unmanageable.

5. On a lightly floured surface, roll out dough to ¼" thick. Don't worry about the square shape.

6. Leaving about a ½" rim around the dough spread the chocolate filling evenly and then sprinkle with the reserved chopped chocolate and pistachios. Make sure to work quickly as it's easier to spread the chocolate filling on chilled dough.

7. Roll the log very tightly. Using a bench scraper, cut the log in half lengthwise and turn the chocolate filling facing up.

8. Braid the two strips with the chocolate filling still facing up.

9. Cut the braid in half so you now have 2 loaves.

10. Put each loaf in a greased parchment-lined bread pan and allow to rise for 4 hours, or overnight in the refrigerator, until the dough has doubled in size.

11. Preheat the oven to 375°F.

12. Bake until golden brown and delicious, about 40 minutes.

13. While baking the dough, combine sugar and water in a small saucepan and bring to boil. Cook for 5 minutes and allow to cool completely to room temperature before brushing on finished Babka.

CHOCOLATE CRANBERRY CHALLAH ROLLS WITH CITRUS SUGAR

Cake for breakfast is meshuggeneh, but challah... eh, live a little. Chocolate and cranberry braided throughout and sprinkled with a citrusy sugar make it a sweet treat perfect for starting the day, nibbling with coffee, or ending a meal.

YIELD: **1 Large Loaf**

ACTIVE TIME: **40 Minutes**

TOTAL TIME: **5 Hours**

CHALLAH

1½ tablespoon dry yeast

½ cup sugar, plus 1 teaspoon, divided

1¼ cups lukewarm water

4½-5 cups all-purpose unbleached flour

½ tablespoon salt

1 teaspoon vanilla

1 teaspoon cinnamon

¼ teaspoon nutmeg

¼ cup vegetable oil

2 eggs

½ cup dark or semi-sweet chocolate chips

½ cup dried cranberries

TOPPING

½ cup sanding sugar

½ tablespoon orange zest

2 egg yolks

1 teaspoon water

1. In a small bowl, combine the yeast, 1 teaspoon sugar, and lukewarm water. Allow to stand for about 10 minutes, until it becomes foamy on top.

2. In the bowl of a stand mixer fitted with the whisk attachment, add 1½ cups flour, salt, the remaining sugar, vanilla, cinnamon, and nutmeg. After the water and yeast mixture has become foamy, add to the flour mixture along with the oil and whisk thoroughly.

3. Add another cup flour and the eggs and mix until smooth. Switch to the dough hook attachment if you are using a stand mixer.

4. Add another 1½ cups flour, mixing thoroughly and then remove from the bowl and place on a floured surface. Knead remaining ½ cup flour into dough, continuing to knead for about 5 minutes. Try not to add too much flour—the less flour you add, the lighter the challah.

5. Place dough in a greased bowl and cover with a damp towel. Allow to rise 3 to 4 hours, punching down at least once if possible.

6. Preheat the oven to 350°F.

7. In a small bowl, combine sanding sugar and orange zest, mix well, and set aside.

8. Braid challah into desired shape (1 large loaf, 2 smaller loaves, or rolls). Allow challah to rise another 45 minutes to 1 hour, or until you can see the size has grown and the challah seems light.

9. In a small bowl, beat the egg yolks with 1 teaspoon water.

10. Brush egg wash liberally over challah and then sprinkle citrus sugar on top.

11. If making one large challah, bake for about 30 minutes; if making two smaller loaves bake for 24 minutes; if making rolls, bake for 22 minutes, or until golden on top.

EGGY CHALLAH TOAST

This combination of sweet coconut milk and herbs creates a surprising and savory twist on a classic.

YIELD: **2 Servings**

ACTIVE TIME: **20 Minutes**

TOTAL TIME: **30 Minutes**

2 eggs

⅓ cup coconut milk

2 tablespoons brown sugar

2 teaspoons soy sauce

2 teaspoons fish sauce

2 garlic cloves, grated

¼ teaspoon turmeric

½ teaspoon kosher salt

1 tablespoon finely chopped cilantro, finely chopped

1 scallion, green tips only, finely chopped

½ teaspoon black pepper

4 slices of day-old challah, ½" cut on diagonal

¼ teaspoon chili oil

1 tablespoon coconut oil

Coconut milk, for serving

Honey, for serving

1. In a bowl, combine the eggs, coconut milk, brown sugar, soy sauce, fish sauce, garlic, turmeric, salt, cilantro, scallions, and black pepper and whisk well.

2. Place the slices of challah in the coconut batter and pierce each piece with a fork a few times to help promote soakage. Let sit for 10 minutes, flipping over several times throughout.

3. Add 1 tablespoon coconut oil to a cast-iron skillet over medium heat. Carefully transfer 2 of the soaked slices to the skillet and lower the heat to medium-low. Cook undisturbed for 2 minutes per side. Repeat with the remaining slices.

4. Enjoy hot with a drizzle of coconut milk and honey.

HONEY BRIOCHE

Top-quality honey makes all the difference here, as it both enriches the flavor of this brioche and helps keep it moist. The brioche is best eaten the day it is baked, although it can be tightly wrapped and stored for a day or two or frozen for up to 1 month; thaw, still wrapped, at room temperature. Make it as a whole loaf or turn it into rolls. Any way you bake it, it's a winner.

YIELD: **2 Batches**

ACTIVE TIME: **35 Minutes**

TOTAL TIME: **7 Hours**

SPONGE

⅓ cup whole milk, lukewarm

1 package (about 2 teaspoons) active dry yeast or instant yeast

1 tablespoon mild, fragrant honey, such as lavender

1 large egg, lightly beaten

2 cups unbleached all-purpose flour

DOUGH

⅓ cup mild, fragrant honey, such as lavender

1 teaspoon fine sea salt

4 large eggs, lightly beaten

1½ cups unbleached all-purpose flour

¾ cup unsalted butter

EGG WASH

1 large egg, lightly beaten

1. Prepare the sponge in the bowl of the heavy-duty mixer by combining the milk, yeast, and honey and stir to blend.

2. Let stand until foamy, about 5 minutes. Add the egg and half the flour and stir to blend. The sponge will be soft and sticky. Sprinkle with the remaining flour to cover the sponge dough, but don't mix it in.

3. Set aside to rest, uncovered, for 30 minutes. The sponge should erupt slightly, cracking the layer of flour. This indicates that the yeast is alive and doing its job.

4. Add the honey, salt, eggs, and flour to the sponge. Mix at low speed just until the ingredients come together, about 1 minute. Increase the mixer speed to medium and beat for 5 minutes.

5. Before adding the butter, it should be the same consistency as the dough. To prepare the butter, place it on a flat work surface, and with the pastry scraper, smear it bit by bit across the surface. (If you do not have a pastry scraper, use the back of a large metal spoon.) When it is ready, the butter should be smooth, soft, but still cool—not warm, oily, or greasy.

6. With the mixer on medium-low speed, add the butter a few table-spoons at a time. When all the butter has been added, increase the mixer speed to medium-high for 1 minute, then reduce the speed to medium and continue to beat for 5 minutes more. The dough will be soft and pliable but shouldn't stick to your hands.

7. Cover the bowl tightly with plastic wrap. Let the dough rise at room temperature until doubled in size, about 2 hours.

8. Punch down the dough. Cover the bowl tightly with plastic wrap and refrigerate the dough overnight, or for at least 4 hours, during which time it should double in size again.

9. Divide the dough into 12 equal pieces, each weighing about 2½ oz. Roll each piece of dough tightly into a ball and place 6 pieces in a bread pan, staggering them in two rows of 3; there will be some space left at either end of the loaf but it will fill up when the dough rises again. Cover the pans with a clean cloth and let the dough rise at room temperature until doubled in size, 1 to 1½ hours.

10. Center a rack in the oven. Preheat the oven to 375°F.

11. Lightly brush the dough with the beaten egg. Working quickly, using the tip of a pair of sharp scissors, snip a cross on the top of each dough ball; this will help the brioche rise evenly as it bakes. Bake until the loaves are puffed and deeply golden, 30 to 35 minutes. Place the pans on a baking rack to cool. Turn the loaves out after they have cooled.

TIP: When using instant yeast, there is no need to let the yeast proof in warm milk; it can be added directly to the flour. Don't omit the milk, however, as this will change the balance of liquid to dry ingredients in the recipe. Instant yeast and active dry yeast can be used interchangeably in the same quantities.

PITA BREAD

Pita is good for everything. It can be stuffed and dipped, heated up and eaten plain.

YIELD: **8 servings**

ACTIVE TIME: **1 Hour**

TOTAL TIME: **3 hours**

1 cup lukewarm water

3 teaspoons dry active yeast

3 teaspoons white sugar

1¾ cups all-purpose white flour

1 cup wheat flour

1 tablespoon kosher salt

1. In a large bowl combine the water, yeast, and sugar. Let sit for 15 minutes or so, until the water is foamy and bubbling. Add the flours and salt, mixing until the flour and water form a dough. Sprinkle with flour when necessary to work the dough. Knead the dough for 1 minute or so, just until the ball is smooth and uniform; it does not need to be kneaded otherwise. Set aside, covered by a towel or plastic wrap, for 2 hours.

2. Preheat the oven to 500°F and place a cast-iron pan or upside-down baking sheet in the oven.

3. Separate the dough into 8 even pieces and ball them up. One at a time, on a floured surface, press the ball down and then, using a rolling pin, roll into a flat surface about ¼" thick.

4. Bake the pitas, 1 at a time. It will take approximately 3 minutes to puff up and 5 minutes or so to brown slightly and be done baking. Serve hot or keep at room temperature.

LAFFA

This flatbread is common across the Middle East and is thicker and chewier than pita. Often served with kebabs and shawarma, it also goes very well with all manner of dips.

YIELD: **8 Servings**

ACTIVE TIME: **30 Minutes**

TOTAL TIME: **1 Hour and 30 Minutes**

1½ cups warm water (about 80°F), divided

2½ teaspoons active dry yeast

2 teaspoons sugar

2 cups all-purpose flour

2 cups bread flour

1 teaspoon sea salt

2 tablespoons olive oil

1. In a bowl, combine the water, yeast, and sugar and let stand until foamy, about 5 to 10 minutes.

2. Combine the all-purpose flour, bread flour, and salt in the bowl of a stand mixer fitted with a dough hook. Mix on low until fully blended.

3. Add yeast mixture, another ½ cup water, and oil and mix on low until a ball forms and pulls away from the sides of the mixer. If after a minute or so a ball is not forming add some more water by the table-spoon to bring it together. The moment the dough ball is pulling away from the bottom and sides of the mixing bowl cleanly, immediately add another ½ cup water and continue to mix until fully incorporated and hydrated. The dough should feel tacky when slapped with a clean hand but it should not be sticky. If it sticks, add a touch more flour, a tablespoon at a time.

4. Cover the dough with plastic wrap and let rise at room temperature until doubled in size, about an hour. Or let it rise in the refrigerator overnight.

5. Set a baking stone or an inverted sheet pan on an oven rack in the upper third of the oven and preheat it to 500°F degrees.

6. Roll the dough into 8 balls the size of baseballs. Cover with a cloth and let rise until they are the size of softballs.

7. Roll each dough ball as thin as possible—less than ⅛" is ideal—on a floured surface using a floured rolling pin.

8. When the dough is rolled out and the hot baking stone is ready, carefully drape one laffa over your hand and stretch, quickly lay the stretched laffa onto the baking stone, quickly pulling any wrinkles flat.

9. Bake laffa until puffy and cooked through, about 1 minute. Serve immediately.

RYE BREAD

Some techniques have changed over the ages, but one thing is for sure: rye is a staple on many a table and is, more often than not, begging to be piled high with corned beef. Before the mid-19th century, all breads were made with sour starters. For Jewish rye bread, the sour rye starter was called roshtshine. To add color, moistness, and a deeper flavor, bakers used an altus or alte brot, old bread.

YIELD: **1 Loaf**

ACTIVE TIME: **55 Minutes**

TOTAL TIME: **3 Hours**

---

1 packet active dry yeast, about 2¼ teaspoons

1¼ cups warm water

2 cups all-purpose flour

1 cup white whole-wheat flour

1 cup rye flour

½ teaspoon sea salt

2 tablespoons brown sugar

2 tablespoons molasses

2 tablespoons canola or grapeseed oil

1 tablespoon caraway seeds

1. In a large bowl, or the mixing bowl of a stand mixer fitted with the dough hook, combine the yeast and water. Let sit until foamy, 5 to 10 minutes. If the yeast doesn't react, discard the mixture and start again with fresh yeast.

2. In another large bowl, whisk together the flours and salt.

3. Add the brown sugar, molasses, oil, and caraway seeds to the yeast mixture. Add 2 cups of the flour mixture, and stir with a wooden spoon or mix on low speed for 1 to 2 minutes, until well blended. Then add the remaining flour.

4. Add the remaining flour, stir the dough well with a wooden spoon, then turn it out onto a lightly floured surface and knead for 5 to 10 minutes, until the dough is smooth, elastic, and slightly tacky. Or mix it with the dough hook for 1 minute on low speed, then 3 to 5 minutes on medium speed, until the dough pulls into a ball and is smooth and slightly tacky but not sticky. Remove the dough hook.

5. If kneading by hand, spread a little oil in the bowl (you don't need to clean it first), and place the dough ball back in the bowl. Cover with a tea towel or plastic wrap and set aside to rise until doubled in size, about 1 hour.

6. Punch down the dough, place on a lightly floured surface, and knead a few times. Shape the dough into a roundish oval, smoothing the top with your hands as you work. Place on a parchment-lined baking pan, cover, and set aside to rise, 45 minutes to 1 hour.

7. Preheat the oven to 350°F.

8. Use a sharp knife to make three or four shallow, diagonal slashes in the top of the loaf. Bake until the loaf is firm, golden on the bottom, and sounds hollow when tapped, about 30 to 35 minutes. Transfer to a rack to cool.

EGG CREAM, page 231

BEVERAGES

With so much food on the table, you need something to wash it down. Here are a few favorites that will be a hit with kids, those feeling nostalgic, and those in the mood for a cocktail.

HAWAIJ HOT COCOA WITH CINNAMON WHIPPED CREAM

A rich, warm, comforting treat to be sipped or slurped with those you consider mishpocheh. The mix of chocolate and cinnamon is a favorite flavor of Mexico.

YIELD: **2 Servings**

ACTIVE TIME: **15 Minutes**

TOTAL TIME: **15 Minutes**

2 cups milk

2 tablespoon sugars

1 oz. dark or semi-sweet chocolate chips or chunks or leftover Hanukkah gelt

1 scant tablespoon cocoa powder

1-2 teaspoons Hawaij Spice Blend

1 pinch salt

Cinnamon Whipped Cream

Cinnamon sticks for garnish (optional)

1. Add milk, sugar, and chocolate to a heavy saucepan over medium-high heat and whisk until chocolate begins to melt.

2. Add cocoa powder, Hawaij Spice Blend, to taste, and salt. Continue to whisk until all chocolate is melted, spices are incorporated, and milk just begins to simmer.

3. Remove from heat and divide the cocoa between 4 mugs. Top with whipped cream and garnish with cinnamon sticks, if desired.

4. Hawaij Spice Blend: In a small bowl, combine 1½ tablespoons ground ginger, 1 tablespoon ground cinnamon, ½ tablespoon ground cardamom, ½ teaspoon ground clove, and 1 pinch nutmeg, mix well, and store in an airtight container.

5. Cinnamon Whipped Cream: Combine 2 cups heavy cream, 2 tablespoons sugar, 1 teaspoon vanilla, and ½ teaspoon cinnamon in a stand mixer fitted with whisk attachment. Place mixer on low setting for 1 minute, then increase to high for 2 to 3 minutes until whipped cream begins to form stiff peaks.

EGG CREAM

Don't let the name fool you, there aren't eggs in this frothy chocolate drink. We'll never know for certain, but the most commonly accepted story about its creation is that Louis Auster made one by accident at the soda fountain of his Brooklyn candy shop, and the rest is rich and creamy history. Be sure to pour one out for Gem Spa in New York City's East Village.

YIELD: **1 Serving**

ACTIVE TIME: **5 Minutes**

TOTAL TIME: **5 Minutes**

3 tablespoons Fox's U-Bet Chocolate Flavor Syrup

¼ cup cold whole milk or half-and-half

13 oz. ice-cold club soda or seltzer water

1. Pour chocolate syrup and milk (or half-and-half) into a pint glass.

2. While beating vigorously with a fork, slowly add club soda until the glass is almost full.

3. Add a straw and serve very cold.

LIMONANA

Israel's classic summer beverage, limonana (a combination of the Hebrew words for lemon and mint) is a refreshing mix of icy lemonade and crushed mint leaves. Ubiquitous in cafés and restaurants throughout the country, this is a summer favorite that is sure to cool you down.

YIELD: **4 Servings**

ACTIVE TIME: **5 Minutes**

TOTAL TIME: **5 Minutes**

1½ cups freshly squeezed lemon juice

3 cups loosely packed mint leaves

1 cup granulated sugar

4 cups water

Ice cubes

1. In a blender, combine the lemon juice, mint, sugar, and ½ cup water and blend until fully liquified.

2. Strain through a fine-mesh sieve, reserving the liquid and discarding the solids.

3. In a pitcher, stir together the mint mixture and the remaining 3 ½ cups water. Serve over ice.

POMEGRANATE PROSECCO PUNCH

Sure, you could just pour a glass of sparkling Prosecco and call it a day, but turning it into a celebratory punch rich with fruity, tart pomegranate juice and citrus takes things in an even livelier direction.

YIELD: **8 Servings**

ACTIVE TIME: **5 Minutes**

TOTAL TIME: **5 Minutes**

1 quart chilled pomegranate juice

2 tablespoons fresh lime juice

¼ cup superfine granulated sugar

2 (750ml) bottles chilled Prosecco

2 clementines, thinly sliced crosswise, for garnish

1 lime, thinly sliced crosswise, for garnish

1. Stir together juices and sugar in a large punch bowl until sugar has dissolved. Stir in Prosecco and serve garnished with fruit.

   TIP: Punch, without Prosecco, can be made 1 day ahead and chilled; add Prosecco when ready to serve.

SACHLAV

With roots in Turkey where it was traditionally made using ground orchid bulbs, in Israel this thick and creamy milk-based drink is served hot and topped with pistachios, grated coconut, and raisins. It's perfect to keep you warm during winter months, and we've been told it's also quite the aphrodisiac... we're already schvitzing.

YIELD: **8 Servings**
ACTIVE TIME: **15 Minutes**
TOTAL TIME: **15 Minutes**

4 cups whole milk
or coconut milk

¼ cup cornstarch

2 teaspoons vanilla extract or
1 vanilla bean, split and seeds
scraped out of the pod

3 tablespoons sugar or honey,
or to taste

1 pinch salt

½ teaspoon rose or orange
blossom water, or to taste

Finely chopped pistachios,
for serving

Shredded coconut, for serving

Ground cinnamon or
cardamom, for serving

1. In a bowl, whisk together ¼ cup milk with the cornstarch to form a slurry.

2. Heat a pot over medium-low heat and add the remaining milk, vanilla, sugar or honey, and salt. Once the milk is hot but is not quite simmering, whisk in the slurry. Continue to whisk or stir the milk with a spoon, until the sweetener completely dissolves into the liquid, and the sachlav thickens enough to coat a spoon, about 3 to 5 minutes. If whisking, your milk will become frothy like a cappuccino, if using a spoon it will thicken more like a custard; either way, make sure the liquid never reaches a boil.

3. Once thickened, remove the sachlav from the heat and add the rose water or orange blossom water. Taste, and add more if desired. If the mixture becomes too thick for your liking, dilute it with a little more milk.

4. Serve the sachlav alongside your desired garnishes.

SEPHARDIC-INSPIRED SANGRIA – TWO WAYS

Wine, spices, and fruity flavors combined into a refreshing drink. What's not to love?

YIELD: **6 Servings**

ACTIVE TIME: **10 Minutes**

TOTAL TIME: **4 Hours**

WHITE PEACH SANGRIA WITH ORANGE BLOSSOM WATER

2 large peaches, pitted and sliced

2 tablespoons light rum

¼ cup simple syrup

2 teaspoons orange blossom water

1 (750ml) bottle white wine (we recommend pinot grigio)

Sparkling water or sparkling wine, for serving

STRAWBERRY ROSÉ SANGRIA

1 cup frozen strawberries

1 cup fresh strawberries, left whole or cut in half

1 red plum, pitted and sliced

2 tablespoons light rum

½ cup sugar

2 teaspoons rose water

1 (750ml) bottle Rosé wine

Sparkling water or sparkling wine, for serving

1. Add 1 peach worth of slices to a blender or food processor with a splash of water and pulse until smooth.

2. In a tall pitcher, add peach puree, sliced peach, rum, simple syrup, orange blossom water, and wine. Mix well and refrigerate for at least 4 hours.

3. When ready to serve, pour into glasses and top with either sparkling wine or sparkling water

Strawberry Rosé Sangria

1. Add the frozen strawberries to a blender or food processor with a splash of water and pulse until smooth.

2. In a tall pitcher, add strawberry puree, simple syrup, fresh strawberries, plum, rum, rose water, and wine. Mix well and refrigerate for at least 4 hours.

3. When ready to serve, pour into glasses and top with either sparkling water or sparkling wine.

SALEP

This warming drink dates back to the Ottoman Empire.

YIELD: **2 Servings**
ACTIVE TIME: **5 Minutes**
TOTAL TIME: **15 Minutes**

2 tablespoons glutinous rice flour

2 cups whole milk

4 teaspoons sugar

¼ teaspoon rose water

Ground cinnamon, for garnish

Finely chopped pistachios, for garnish

1. Add rice flour and milk to a small saucepan over medium heat and bring to a simmer, whisking constantly to avoid clumping.

2. When the mixture has thickened, about 2 minutes longer, add sugar and rose water and stir until sugar dissolves completely.

3. Divide salep between two mugs and garnish with cinnamon and pistachios.

APPENDIX

CHICKEN STOCK

YIELD: 6 Quarts
ACTIVE TIME: 20 Minutes
TOTAL TIME: 6 to 7 Hours

10 lbs. chicken carcasses and/or stewing chicken pieces

½ cup vegetable oil

1 leek, trimmed and carefully washed, cut into 1" pieces

1 large yellow onion, unpeeled, root cleaned, cut into 1" pieces

2 large carrots, cut into 1" pieces

1 celery stalk with leaves, cut into 1" pieces

10 quarts water

8 fresh sprigs parsley

5 fresh sprigs thyme

2 bay leaves

1 teaspoon peppercorns

1 teaspoon salt

1. Preheat the oven to 350°F.

2. Lay the bones on a flat baking tray, place in the oven, and cook for 30 to 45 minutes, until they are golden brown. Remove and set aside.

3. Meanwhile, in a large stockpot, add the oil and warm over low heat. Add the vegetables and cook until any additional moisture has evaporated. This allows the flavor of the vegetables to become concentrated.

4. Add the water to the stockpot. Add the chicken carcasses and/or stewing pieces, the aromatics, the peppercorns, and the salt to the stockpot, raise heat to high, and bring to a boil.

5. Reduce heat so that the stock simmers and cook for a minimum of 2 hours. Skim fat and impurities from the top as the stock cooks. Cook until the desired flavor is achieved, around 4 to 5 hours.

6. When the stock is finished cooking, strain through a fine strainer or cheesecloth. Place stock in the refrigerator to chill.

7. Once cool, skim the fat layer from the top and discard. Use immediately, refrigerate, or freeze.

VEAL, BEEF, OR LAMB STOCK

YIELD: 6 Quarts
ACTIVE TIME: 30 Minutes
TOTAL TIME: 6 to 7 Hours

10 lbs. veal, beef, or lamb bones

½ cup vegetable oil

1 leek, trimmed and carefully washed, cut into 1" pieces

1 large yellow onion, unpeeled, root cleaned, cut into 1" pieces

2 large carrots, peeled and cut into 1" pieces

1 celery stalk with leaves, cut into 1" pieces

10 quarts water

8 fresh sprigs parsley

5 fresh sprigs thyme

2 bay leaves

1 teaspoon peppercorns

1 teaspoon salt

1 cup tomato paste

1. Preheat oven to 350°F.

2. Lay the bones on a flat baking tray, place in the oven, and cook for 30 to 45 minutes, until they are golden brown. Remove and set aside.

3. Meanwhile, in a large stockpot, add the oil and warm over low heat. Add the vegetables and cook until any additional moisture has evaporated. This allows the flavor of the vegetables to become concentrated.

4. Add the water to the stockpot. Add the bones, aromatics, peppercorns, salt, and tomato paste to the stockpot, raise heat to high, and bring to a boil.

5. Reduce heat so that the stock simmers and cook for a minimum of 2 hours. Skim fat and impurities from the top as the stock cooks. Cook until the desired flavor is achieved, around 4 to 5 hours.

6. When the stock is finished cooking, strain through a fine strainer or cheesecloth. Place the stock in the refrigerator to chill.

7. Once cool, skim the fat layer from the top and discard. Use immediately, refrigerate, or freeze.

VEGETABLE STOCK

YIELD: 6 Cups
ACTIVE TIME: 20 Minutes
TOTAL TIME: 3 Hours

2 tablespoons vegetable oil

2 large leeks, trimmed and carefully washed

2 large carrots, peeled and sliced

2 celery stalks, sliced

2 large onions, sliced

3 garlic cloves, unpeeled and smashed

2 fresh sprigs parsley

2 fresh sprigs thyme

1 bay leaf

8 cups water

½ teaspoon black peppercorns

Salt, to taste

1. In a large stockpot, add the oil and the vegetables and cook over low heat until any additional moisture has evaporated. This will allow the flavor of the vegetables to become concentrated.

2. Add the aromatics, water, peppercorns, and salt. Raise heat to high and bring to a boil. Reduce heat so that the soup simmers and cook for 2 hours. Skim fat and impurities from the top as the stock cooks.

3. When the stock is finished cooking, strain through a fine strainer or cheesecloth. Place the stock in the refrigerator to chill.

4. Once cool, skim the fat layer from the top and discard. Use immediately, refrigerate, or freeze.

GRIBENES & SCHMALTZ

YIELD: ½ cup Schmaltz / 2 cups Gribenes
ACTIVE TIME: 15 Minutes
TOTAL TIME: 1 Hour and 30 Minutes

¾ lb. chicken skin and fat, diced (use scissors, or freeze then dice with a knife)

¾ teaspoon kosher salt

½ medium onion, peeled and cut into ¼" slices

1. In a large nonstick skillet over medium heat, toss chicken skin and fat with salt and 1 tablespoon water and spread out in one layer. Cook over medium heat for about 15 minutes, until fat starts to render and skin begins to turn golden at the edges.

2. Add onion, if using, and cook 45 minutes to 1 hour longer, tossing occasionally, until chicken skin and onions are crispy and richly browned, but not burned.

3. Strain through a sieve. Reserve the Schmaltz and store in refrigerator for up to 6 months.

4. If you want the gribenes to be crispier, return to the skillet and cook over high heat until done to taste. Drain gribenes on a paper-towel-lined plate before serving

BERBERE SPICE MIX

YIELD: 8 oz.
ACTIVE TIME: 5 Minutes
TOTAL TIME: 5 Minutes

1 cup hot paprika or chile powder
½ tablespoon ground cloves
1 tablespoon ground cardamom
1 tablespoon ginger powder
1 tablespoon onion powder
1 tablespoon coriander
1 tablespoon cumin
½ tablespoon cinnamon
½ tablespoon ground nutmeg
½ tablespoon ground fenugreek seeds
1 tablespoon black pepper
1 tablespoon sea salt

1. Sift all of the spices into a bowl, mix well, and set aside.

ZA'ATAR

YIELD: 8 oz.
ACTIVE TIME: 5 Minutes
TOTAL TIME: 5 Minutes

1 tablespoon cumin
1 tablespoon sumac
1 tablespoon thyme
2 teaspoons hemp seeds
2 teaspoons crushed toasted sunflower seeds
2 tablespoons sesame seeds
2 tablespoons sea salt
1 tablespoon black pepper
2 tablespoons oregano
2 tablespoons basil
2 tablespoons parsley
1 tablespoon garlic powder
1 tablespoon onion powder

1. In a large mixing bowl, combine all of the ingredients and mix thoroughly.

GREEN ZHOUG

YIELD: 20 oz.
ACTIVE TIME: 10 Minutes
TOTAL TIME: 10 Minutes

4 jalapeños, stems removed

2 cups parsley

¼ cup cilantro

6 mint leaves

1 onion, rough chopped

5 garlic cloves

Juice of 1 lemon

1 tablespoon kosher salt

½ cup extra virgin olive oil

¼ cup water

1. Cut the jalapeños into 5 pieces each. Place the peppers, parsley, cilantro, mint, onion, garlic and lemon juice into a food processor and pulse until all ingredients are combined and rough chopped.

2. Add the salt and, while on high, slowly pour in the olive oil. If the mixture doesn't blend smoothly, add the water to help it along. The finished product should be the texture of a chimichurri and it will keep in the refrigerator for up to 1 week.

CONVERSION TABLE

WEIGHTS

1 oz. = 28 grams

2 oz. = 57 grams

4 oz. (¼ lb.) = 113 grams

8 oz. (½ lb.) = 227 grams

16 oz. (1 lb.) = 454 grams

VOLUME MEASURES

⅛ teaspoon = 0.6 ml

¼ teaspoon = 1.23 ml

½ teaspoon = 2.5 ml

1 teaspoon = 5 ml

1 tablespoon (3 teaspoons) = ½ fluid oz. = 15 ml

2 tablespoons = 1 fluid oz. = 29.5 ml

¼ cup (4 tablespoons) = 2 fluid oz. = 59 ml

⅓ cup (5 ⅓ tablespoons) = 2.7 fluid oz. = 80 ml

½ cup (8 tablespoons) = 4 fluid oz. = 120 ml

⅔ cup (10 ⅔ tablespoons) = 5.4 fluid oz. = 160 ml

¾ cup (12 tablespoons) = 6 fluid oz. = 180 ml

1 cup (16 tablespoons) = 8 fluid oz. = 240 ml

TEMPERATURE EQUIVALENTS

°F	°C	Gas Mark
225	110	¼
250	130	½
275	140	1
300	150	2
325	170	3
350	180	4
375	190	5
400	200	6
425	220	7
450	230	8
475	240	9
500	250	10

LENGTH MEASURES

1/16 inch = 1.6 mm

⅛ inch = 3 mm

¼ inch = 1.35 mm

½ inch = 1.25 cm

¾ inch = 2 cm

1 inch = 2.5 cm

INDEX

ABOUT CIDER MILL PRESS BOOK PUBLISHERS

Good ideas ripen with time. From seed to harvest, Cider Mill Press brings fine reading, information, and entertainment together between the covers of its creatively crafted books. Our Cider Mill bears fruit twice a year, publishing a new crop of titles each spring and fall.

"Where Good Books Are Ready for Press"

Visit us online at
cidermillpress.com

or write to us at
PO Box 454
12 Spring St.
Kennebunkport, Maine 04046